NEW MERMAIDS

General editors:
William C. Carroll, Boston University
Brian Gibbons, University of Münster
Tiffany Stern, University of Oxford

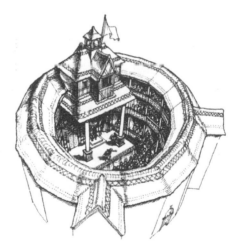

Reconstruction of an Elizabethan theatre
by C. Walter Hodges

NEW MERMAIDS

CHRISTOPHER MARLOWE

EDWARD THE SECOND

edited by Martin Wiggins

Fellow of the Shakespeare Institute
University of Birmingham

and

Robert Lindsey

Oriel College, Oxford

Methuen Drama • London

New Mermaids

9 10 8

Published by Methuen Drama, an imprint of Bloomsbury Publishing Plc

Methuen Drama
Bloomsbury Publishing Plc
50 Bedford Square
London WC1B 3DP
www.methuendrama.com

First New Mermaid edition 1967
copyright © Ernest Benn Limited 1967

Second Edition 1997
Reprinted with a new cover design in 2003, 2005, 2006, 2009

ISBN: 978 0 7136 6669 4

A CIP catalogue record for this book is available from the British Library

Available in the USA from Bloomsbury Academic & Professional, 175 Fifth
Avenue/3rd Floor, New York, NY 10010. www.BloomsburyAcademicUSA.com

Printed and bound in Great Britain

CONTENTS

PREFACE AND ACKNOWLEDGEMENTS

The Introduction to this edition is the work of Martin Wiggins; the text and commentary were prepared by Robert Lindsey and Martin Wiggins in collaboration. Our paramount debt is to the General Editor, Brian Gibbons, whose painstaking and exacting work has significantly improved the edition, especially in matters on which we ultimately had to agree to differ. In the early stages of preparing the edition, Dr L. G. Black gave valuable advice and guidance, Simon Markham made useful suggestions on the text and notes, and Roma Gill gave both encouragement and the benefit of her knowledge and experience. In the later stages, we have further benefited from the textual expertise of John Jowett and the wisdom of Stanley Wells. We have been fortunate in dealing with librarians and archivists who fully understand the needs of the researcher, particularly Susan Brock of the Shakespeare Institute Library, Stratford-upon-Avon; James Shaw of the Shakespeare Centre Library, Stratford-upon-Avon; Susan Knowles of the BBC Written Archives Centre, Caversham; and Richard Bell of the Bodleian Library, Oxford. Among postgraduate students, Rebekah Owens shared the results of her research on Kyd's letter to Puckering, and Solitaire Townsend, Shaalu Malhotra, and Sue Taylor all helped to locate material relating to the stage history. Paul Edmondson, Jeremy Ehrlich, Eugene Giddens, Mary McGuigan, and especially Jane Kingsley-Smith made an invaluable contribution to the proof-checking. At A. & C. Black, Anne Watts has been a supportive and sympathetic editor, and we could not have hoped for a better job of copy-editing than we received from Margaret Berrill. Others who have helped in various ways, great and small, are Kelley Costigan, Lorna Flint, Andrew Pixley, Trefor Stockwell, Keith Topping, and The Malone Society.

ABBREVIATIONS

Editions of the Play Cited

Bevington and Rasmussen	*Doctor Faustus and Other Plays*, ed. David Bevington and Eric Rasmussen (Oxford, 1995)
Briggs	*Edward II*, ed. William Dinsmore Briggs (London, 1914)
Charlton and Waller	*Edward II*, ed. H. B. Charlton and R. D. Waller (London, 1933)
Forker	*Edward the Second*, ed. Charles R. Forker, The Revels Plays (Manchester and New York, 1994)
Gill	*Edward II*, ed. Roma Gill (London, 1967)
Merchant	*Edward the Second*, ed. W. Moelwyn Merchant, New Mermaids (London, 1967)
Rowland	*The Complete Works of Christopher Marlowe*, vol. III: *Edward II*, ed. Richard Rowland (Oxford, 1994)

Periodicals and Reference Works

Dent	R. W. Dent, *Shakespeare's Proverbial Language: An Index* (Berkeley, 1981)
MLN	*Modern Language Notes*
N&Q	*Notes and Queries*
Tilley	Morris Palmer Tilley (ed.), *A Dictionary of the Proverbs in England in the Sixteenth and Seventeenth Centuries* (Ann Arbor, 1950)

Other plays of Marlowe are quoted from Bevington and Rasmussen and from *'Dido Queen of Carthage' and 'The Massacre at Paris'*, ed. H. J. Oliver, The Revels Plays (London, 1968). Shakespeare is quoted from *The Complete Works*, ed. Stanley Wells, Gary Taylor, John Jowett, and William Montgomery (Oxford, 1986). Other editions quoted are Thomas Lodge, *The Wounds of Civil War*, ed. Joseph W. Houppert, Regents Renaissance Drama (Lincoln, Nebr., 1969), and George Peele, *Edward I*, ed. Frank S. Hook, in *The Dramatic Works of George Peele*, gen. ed. Charles Tyler Prouty (New Haven and London, 1961).

INTRODUCTION

THE AUTHOR

Christopher Marlowe, the first son of Canterbury shoemaker John Marlowe and his wife Katherine, was baptized on 26 February 1564, in the same year that John became a freeman of the city. As a child, he grew up among sisters: though his elder sibling Mary (b. 1562) died when he was only four years old, the Marlowes produced four more girls before completing their family with a second son, Thomas (b. 1576).[1] The surviving local records show that John Marlowe was a difficult and improvident man, repeatedly prosecuted for debt, but Christopher was fortunate in being elected to a scholarship at the King's School, Canterbury, at the end of 1578. Less than two years later a further scholarship, this one endowed by the late Archbishop of Canterbury, Matthew Parker, took him to Corpus Christi College, Cambridge, as a potential aspirant to the Anglican clergy.

Marlowe matriculated in March 1581, and passed his B.A. examinations in February 1584. The College buttery book indicates that he was intermittently away from Cambridge, and these absences seem to have become more pronounced during the period of his candidacy for the M.A. Rumours circulated that he 'was determined to have gone beyond the seas to Rheims and there to remain'.[2] This was a more serious matter than simply failing to observe the University's residence requirements: at a time when England was heading for open war with the Roman Catholic powers on the Continent, Marlowe was being accused of defecting to the enemy. The seminary at Rheims in France trained religious missionaries for the reconversion of Protestant England, but the English authorities saw it as a training ground for sedition and subversion. Not surprisingly, the University was reluctant to allow Marlowe to proceed to his M.A.

What followed is perhaps the most tantalizingly mysterious event of Marlowe's life. On 29 June 1587, the Privy Council wrote to the Cambridge authorities, denying that he had intended to become a

---

[1] The four sisters were Margaret (1565–?1641), Jane (1569–?83), Anne (1571–1652), and Dorothy (b. 1573). Two baby boys were born in 1568 and 1570 respectively, but both died soon afterwards.

[2] *Acts of the Privy Council*, n.s. xv. 141.

seminarist, and certifying 'that in all his actions he had behaved himself orderly and discreetly, whereby he had done Her Majesty good service'. Their lordships brought to bear the strongest possible pressure in support of their request that Marlowe should be granted his degree and gossip about his activities 'be allayed by all possible means': 'it was not Her Majesty's pleasure that anyone employed, as he had been, in matters touching the benefit of his country should be defamed by those that are ignorant in th' affairs he went about'.[3] The exact nature of those affairs has exercised the imagination of many a biographer, and the figure of Marlowe the spy has entered literary folklore; but unless further documentary evidence is unearthed, all that can confidently be said is that the absent student was engaged in activity of a secret nature, possibly overseas, and possibly touching on national security. In any event, the University relented, and Marlowe took his degree that summer; he never presented himself for ordination.

By this time he had already completed his first play, and perhaps also his second. In collaboration with his Cambridge contemporary Thomas Nashe he had written the tragedy *Dido, Queen of Carthage* (c. 1586) for the Children of the Chapel, but it was his barnstorming *Tamburlaine the Great* (1587) which sealed his success as a playwright: he was promptly commissioned to write a sequel, *The Second Part of Tamburlaine*, and for the rest of the sixteenth century it was these two plays which were reckoned to mark the beginning of modern drama. Four more tragedies followed, all for the adult companies and their open-air amphitheatres: *Doctor Faustus* (c. 1588), *The Jew of Malta* (c. 1589), *The Massacre at Paris*, and *Edward the Second* (both c. 1591–2). This brief writing career was framed by two important non-dramatic works: an unexpurgated, sexually explicit translation of Ovid's *Amores*, probably written at Cambridge and surreptitiously published after Marlowe's death; and an erotic epyllion, *Hero and Leander* (1593), generally thought to have been composed at Sir Thomas Walsingham's house at Scadbury in Kent after plague had closed the London theatres.

After leaving Cambridge, Marlowe was repeatedly in trouble with the law. In September 1589 he spent nearly two weeks in Newgate Prison after becoming embroiled in a London street fight which ended in a man's death, while 1592 saw him, in January, arrested in Flushing in the Low Countries after being caught, with others, counterfeiting coins; in May, bound over after a scuffle with two London constables; and, in September, sued for assault after a violent attack on a tailor in Canterbury. Finally, yet another fight, in Deptford on 30 May 1593, saw him stabbed to death by Ingram

[3] Ibid.

Frizer, a confidence trickster – though there is no evidence for the traditional supposition that this was a 'tavern brawl'.[4]

By this time Marlowe's clashes with authority had taken a more serious turn. Less than a fortnight earlier, he had been summoned for examination by the Privy Council, which was growing concerned about the circulation of subversive and heretical material in London. His name had come up several times in this connection: xenophobic verses posted on the Dutch church in London had associated themselves with his character, Tamburlaine; and the playwright Thomas Kyd, arrested after a heterodox document was found among his papers, named Marlowe as its author. Most damaging was evidence submitted by Marlowe's former associate Richard Baines, in which it was alleged, among other shocking charges, that he attacked the historicity of the Bible and the divinity of Jesus, and did his best to convert people to atheism. Evidently the dramatist was coming to be regarded by some as a dangerous free-thinker; and there has been no shortage of conspiracy theorists suggesting that there was something more than his well-documented quarrelsome streak behind his death in Deptford.

Nobody knows how reliable an informer Baines was, but two of the opinions he attributed to Marlowe are particularly relevant to *Edward the Second*: that Jesus and St John were lovers, and 'that all they that love not tobacco and boys were fools'.[5] Given that his plays and poems frequently touch on homosexual love, from the pederasty of the classical gods in *Dido, Queen of Carthage* and *Hero and Leander* to the affairs of European monarchs in *The Massacre at Paris* and *Edward the Second*, it is sometimes confidently asserted that the dramatist was himself gay. Less often remarked is the explicit heterosexuality of characters like Tamburlaine and Faustus and the 'heteroeroticism' of the translation of Ovid. Undoubtedly sexuality, of all varieties, is a recurrent concern of Marlowe's work; but the question of his own sexuality remains, at best, ambiguous.

DATE, SOURCE, AND PRODUCTIONS

There is little adducible internal or external evidence from which the composition of *Edward the Second* may be dated. The play is normally assigned to 1592, on the basis of a qualitative, and therefore subjective, judgement of its maturity in comparison with the rest of the Marlowe canon. One reason for the lack of more con-

[4] William Urry, *Christopher Marlowe and Canterbury* (London and Boston, 1988), pp. 83–4.
[5] Millar MacLure (ed.), *Marlowe: The Critical Heritage, 1588–1896* (London, Boston, and Henley, 1979), p. 37.

crete evidence is the nature of the play as an historical tragedy: there is less room for topical allusion in a play whose content is determined primarily by source material rather than by the author's originary invention. The narrative sources themselves have little bearing on the question of the date: none of them would have been unavailable to Marlowe at any time in the six years he was writing for the professional adult theatre. Principal among them was the account of Edward II's reign in Raphael Holinshed's *Chronicles of England, Scotland, and Ireland*; Marlowe probably used the second edition, published in the year he went down from Cambridge, 1587. He seems to have done his research diligently, for in addition he consulted two or three other substantial history books: from Robert Fabyan's *Chronicle* (1559) he took the Scottish 'jig' derisively quoted by the Earl of Lancaster in Scene 6, while John Stow's *Chronicles of England* (1580) supplied the episode in Scene 22 in which Edward is washed and shaved in puddle water; some minor details suggest that he had also read Richard Grafton's *Chronicle* (1569).[6]

The broader imaginative influences on Marlowe are more suggestive but harder to pin down. At the time, the portrayal of a homosexual king excessively devoted to 'favourites' must have had resonances of Henry III of France, who had been assassinated in 1587; Henry features prominently in Marlowe's sensational tragedy of recent French history, *The Massacre at Paris*, probably written in either 1591 or 1593, and arguably *Edward the Second*'s closest relative in the Marlowe canon. The play's political concerns, moreover, are characteristic of the historical tragedies of the early 1590s: civil strife between a weak king and his barons, ultimately leading to deposition, was a recurrent theme in such plays as Shakespeare's *Henry VI* (1591) and the anonymous *Thomas of Woodstock* (c. 1592), before receiving its greatest exposition in Shakespeare's *King Richard II* (1595), itself much influenced by Marlowe.[7]

Lightborne, the professional assassin who murders Edward with such appalling inventiveness, is the principal character who is unequivocally Marlowe's invention, with no original in the narrative sources; and as such he has some bearing on the dating. Hired killers became increasingly commonplace in early 1590s drama, and Lightborne has a particularly close relative in the artisanal murderer who appears at the climax of *Thomas of Woodstock* – though it

---

[6] For a thorough analysis of Marlowe's transformation of his narrative sources, see Forker, pp. 41–66.

[7] For a fuller account of this genre, see Michael Manheim, *The Weak King Dilemma in the Shakespearean History Play* (Syracuse, N.Y., 1973). On Shakespeare's debt to Marlowe, see Nicholas Brooke, 'Marlowe as Provocative Agent in Shakespeare's Early Plays', *Shakespeare Survey* 14 (1961), 34–44.

is hard to say which play influenced which.[8] In his Italianate qualities, however, he is an entirely original creation, and this may anchor the play more firmly in 1592, when Marlowe's former collaborator Thomas Nashe memorably dubbed Italy 'the academy of manslaughter'.[9] More particularly, the turn of the year had seen a security scare about a specialist Italian 'executioner' supposedly being sent from the Low Countries to assassinate the Queen. Both this case and the year's broader anti-Italian feeling could lie behind Marlowe's distinctive killer.[10]

The play was performed by the Earl of Pembroke's Men, a troupe whose existence is first recorded in 1592, and whose financial difficulties the following year forced them to release several of their plays, including *Edward the Second*, for publication. The title-page claims that it 'was sundry times publicly acted in the honourable city of London', but it is not known at which play-house, and, as with all sixteenth-century drama, our knowledge of the production is largely inferential. By modern standards the staging would have been relatively minimalist. The action would have taken place without scenery, against the permanent architecture of the theatre, and the performers would have entered the stage through two or more doors set into the back wall, sometimes using different doors to signify different directions; in Scene 24 Edward would probably have come up from his dungeon through a trap in the stage floor. Beyond that, there is no call for multi-level staging, and the demand for props is modest, with little more than the crown, severed head, and the like, which are the standard requirement of many an Elizabethan tragedy.

We are scarcely better informed about early audiences' reception of the play. Evidently it was at least popular enough to be considered worth offering for sale in print, and presumably continued to do reasonable business for its publishers over the next thirty years, during which three more editions appeared. However, there were no theatre reviews in Elizabethan London to record a more detailed response. Occasionally it is possible to infer something from a contemporary allusion to the events of a play, but in this case there is the problem of differentiating between Marlowe's version and the original historical subject-matter. It is only to be expected, then, that the one piece of unambiguously relevant material should deal with Lightborne, the subject of a curious little epigram probably written early in the seventeenth century:

---

[8] Martin Wiggins, *Journeymen in Murder: The Assassin in English Renaissance Drama* (Oxford, 1991), p. 123.

[9] Thomas Nashe, *Pierce Penniless*, in *The Works of Thomas Nashe*, ed. R. B. McKerrow, 2nd ed. (Oxford, 1958), vol. 1, p. 186.

[10] For a fuller account, see Wiggins, *Journeymen in Murder*, pp. 49–52.

Here lieth Lightborne dead in a ditch,
Begot between the Devil and a witch.
All you that know him do him the grace,
So down with your hose and shit in his face.[11]

The King's murderer was evidently a memorable, and dislikable figure.

The play's first theatrical life extended into the 1620s at the rowdy, plebeian Red Bull playhouse in Clerkenwell; but after the closure of the theatres during the interregnum, it seems to have disappeared from the stage. In 1781, it was a 'forgotten tragedy', available for reading only in antiquarian anthologies.[12] Literary critics of the nineteenth century frequently called it Marlowe's best play, but it was not until 1903 that it received its first stage revival, in an amateur production directed by William Poel for the Elizabethan Stage Society; the title role was taken by Harley Granville Barker.[13] The first professional production since the seventeenth century followed in 1905, in a much abridged version as part of the Shakespeare Festival at Stratford-upon-Avon; perhaps surprisingly, Edward was played by the Festival's manly, cricketing founder, Frank Benson, who also directed. Further major productions were directed by Alan Wade for the Phoenix Society in 1923, with Duncan Yarrow as the King, and by Joan Littlewood for her radical Theatre Workshop group in 1956. Broadcasting has served the play well: there have been numerous radio versions, beginning with a live performance in 1931, and it was televised for the first time on 30 October 1947, with Stephen Harrison directing David Markham's Edward; the cast also included Nigel Stock as Kent and Patrick Troughton as Baldock. It has also been popular with amateur actors, particularly student drama groups, and 1958 saw a notable Marlowe Society production with John Barton as Mortimer Junior.

There have been a number of adaptations over the years; the play has even been turned into a ballet by David Bintley, which premiered at Stuttgart in 1995. Perhaps the most notable reworking was written in 1924 by Bertolt Brecht and Lion Feuchtwanger, after Brecht, producing the play at Munich, could find no other way of avoiding 'the Shakespearean tradition common to German theatres: that lumpy monumental style beloved of middle-class philistines'.[14] The result was a vulgarized comic treatment of Marlowe's text which had a long stage life in its own right, includ-

---

[11] Oxford: Bodleian Library, MS Rawl. poet. 160, fo. 163^v, quoted by Rowland, p. xxxii.

[12] MacLure, Marlowe: The Critical Heritage, p. 60.

[13] Ibid., pp. 80, 87, 94, 104, 115, 163, 166.

[14] Bertolt Brecht, Collected Plays (London, 1970), vol. 1, p. 454.

ing a National Theatre production in 1968.[15] Derek Jarman's film
version of 1991 was an even more radical adaptation in a pseudo-
modern setting: portraying the Queen and barons as repressed establishment figures, it was strongly sympathetic to Edward and
Gaveston; Jarman himself admitted that his primary concern was
'to make a film of a gay love affair', and that using Marlowe's 'dusty
old play' as a starting-point was only a device to get it commissioned.[16]

Mainstream productions in England since the late 1960s have
also given especial emphasis to the play's homosexual overtones;
the title role has tended to interest avowedly gay actors such as
Simon Russell Beale and, in 1995, the transvestite comedian Eddie
Izzard. Ian McKellen was Edward in Toby Robertson's celebrated
1969 production for the Prospect Theatre Company, supported by
James Laurenson as Gaveston, Timothy West as Mortimer Junior,
and Diane Fletcher as the Queen. McKellen's Edward engaged in
an unprecedented degree of physical intimacy with his courtiers,
and when the production was broadcast the following year, it was
the first time homosexual kissing had been seen on British television.[17] Subsequent productions were even more explicitly homoerotic: both Nicholas Hytner's 1986 production at the Manchester
Royal Exchange with Ian McDiarmid as Edward, and the Royal
Shakespeare Company's production at the Swan Theatre four years
later, inserted spicy versions of the 'lascivious shows' (6. 154) with
which Edward and Gaveston entertain themselves, and the RSC's
King (Simon Russell Beale) and his lovers wore studded leather
costumes and pert codpieces, the latter constantly at eye-level for
the ground-floor audience thanks to a raised stage. A discreet notice outside the Swan warned playgoers that the production might
'not be suitable for children'.

SEXUALITY

The late twentieth century has seen *Edward the Second* hailed as a
'gay classic'. So prominent has this aspect of the play become that
rumours persist – they are inevitably hard to verify – that in some
parts of Britain it was banned from school syllabuses during the late

---

[15] For a fuller analysis of this version of the play, see Louise J. Laboulle, 'A Note on
Bertold Brecht's Adaptation of Marlowe's *Edward II*', *Modern Language Review*
54 (1959), 214–20.

[16] Derek Jarman, *Queer Edward II* (London, 1991), p. iii. The film was commissioned by the BBC and, after a limited cinema release, was televised on 24
January 1993.

[17] The programme was transmitted on 6 August 1970; an archive recording exists at
the BBC.

1980s and early 1990s under the infamous anti-AIDS Clause 28 of the Conservative government's local government legislation, which prohibited public bodies from supporting works of art that condoned homosexual behaviour. 'In the Mercutio/Romeo relationship, and in *Coriolanus*, you can ignore the homosexual content if you so choose,' commented Gerard Murphy, director of the 1990 RSC production; 'You *can't* in *Edward II*.'[18]

The point is broadly valid, even if the text itself does not call for the degree of overt physical homosexuality seen in the more recent stagings. The parameters are set in the play's opening speech, when Gaveston compares his relationship with Edward to one of the famous love stories of classical legend:

> Sweet prince, I come; these, these thy amorous lines
> Might have enforced me to have swum from France,
> And, like Leander, gasped upon the sand,
> So thou wouldst smile and take me in thy arms. (1. 6–9)

The parallel tacitly establishes that this is more than just the Renaissance male friendship seen in, for example, *The Two Gentlemen of Verona*: Leander's nightly meeting with Hero after his swim across the Hellespont was specifically a union of sexual love, and Marlowe later portrayed it as such in his *Hero and Leander*; the association helps to give an erotic edge to Gaveston's gasping breaths and Edward's smiling embrace. The classically-educated Elizabethans would not have missed the point: King Edward and Piers Gaveston are lovers.

The play must have been as challenging and disturbing in its own time as it remains to the illiberal elements in today's society. The official culture of the 1590s was exceptionally intolerant towards what it perceived as deviant sexuality. Moralists and theologians held that God did not create sex for recreational purposes, for human pleasure; rather sex enabled mankind to procreate, to people the world with God-fearing Christians. The choice of sexual partner, and the mode of intercourse, was not simply a private issue or a matter of taste: buggery was held to be a sin against God, in that the participants took pleasure in a sexual act that, contrary to God's intention, could not lead to conception. This was considered sufficiently heinous for such acts to have a specific legal status, like the sins of murder and theft: in Marlowe's England, sodomy was a capital offence.

The play's challenge lies not only in that it implicates the King of England in such a crime, but also in allowing its audience to adopt attitudes more complex than a simple univocal condemnation of

---

[18] Gerard Murphy, quoted by Terence Michael Stephenson, 'Sweet Lies', *Gay Times*, August 1990, 34.

the errant monarch. Until the very end of the play, admittedly, Edward is a largely unsympathetic character; but it is not his homosexuality in itself which makes him so. His devotion to his lover is single-minded and obsessive, and this makes his behaviour to everyone else abominably insensitive. Gaveston is piled with titles, and supplants even the King's closest associates: Edward seats him by his side in the Queen's place (4. 8), and calls him 'brother' (6. 35), in the presence of his actual brother, the Earl of Kent. It is this stupid disregard for other people's feelings that costs him the support both of potential allies and of the audience; and in this respect Gaveston makes a telling contrast. In the opening scene, for example, he responds encouragingly to the poor men's request for employment, even though he has no intention of meeting it:

> it is no pain to speak men fair;
> I'll flatter these, and make them live in hope.   (1. 41-2)

As the King's boyfriend, he is in an exposed position, bound to give offence to some people whatever he does; but it is clear that he recognizes the crucial political importance of good public relations. The same contrast informs the two men's handling of their marital relationships. Gaveston can dissimulate heterosexual love-talk when needs be: in the course of his liaison with Edward he also finds time to woo and wed Edward's niece, Margaret de Clare. She seems a contented and loyal wife, never supposing that he is not her 'sweet Gaveston' (5. 59), and when he has to leave the court and Edward in Scene 8, she goes with him. Edward's relationship with his Queen is rockier. Gaveston characteristically advises that he should 'dissemble with her, speak her fair' (6. 226), but doing so goes against the grain: Edward generally treats her with a contemptuous neglect which forces her successively into emotional isolation, exile, and finally adultery.

In performance, our sense of the differences between Edward and Gaveston can be affected by the age at which the roles are cast. Several productions have treated their relationship in terms of a middle-aged man's fascination with a pretty boy: both Frank Benson in 1905 and Ian McDiarmid in 1986 were a generation older than their respective Gavestons, Clarence Derwent and Michael Grandage.[19] There have also been Gavestons in their forties, such as Ernest Thesiger in 1923 and Alan Wheatley in 1947. In many respects, however, *Edward the Second* is a young man's play, appropriate for the student actors with whom it has been popular: Edward himself has been played by distinguished undergraduates from Derek Jacobi in the 1958 Marlowe Society produc-

---

[19] Derwent, born on 23 March 1884, turned twenty-one only a month before Benson's production opened. Benson was forty-six.

tion to Tony Slattery in the 1980s. Practical considerations add to the case for casting the role young: its physical and emotional demands require an actor of great stamina and courage. (It is said to have given Peter Smallwood, Joan Littlewood's Edward, a breakdown which forced him to retire from the profession.)[20] '*Lear* is a far greater play,' commented Simon Russell Beale early in the run of the 1990 RSC production, 'But for sheer concentrated self-flagellation, *Edward* takes some beating. Every emotional step you take has to be done fullbloodedly.'[21]

Having a younger Edward in performance helps to focus several aspects of the text. The emphasis is on a new generation coming to power and prominence: it is symptomatic that Mortimer Junior and Spencer Junior are both more important characters than their respective Seniors. King Edward I, Edward's father and Gaveston's original banisher, is newly dead as the action begins (the 1990 RSC production underlined the point by showing the funeral in dumb show), and the next King's accession to the throne is also his accession to sexual freedom: 'My father is deceased; come, Gaveston,' (1. 1) reads his letter which opens the play.

If Edward has attained legal majority, however, psychological maturity eludes him: in politics and passion alike, as we have seen, he still has a boyish absolutism similar to that of Shakespeare's Coriolanus – determined to be faithful to one person, determined never to compromise his true feelings. The paradox is that although Edward is unequivocally the play's leading role, the emphasis on his immaturity means that he is constantly overshadowed: 'Was ever king thus overruled as I?' (4. 38), he petulantly demands at the first crisis of his reign. The play sandwiches him between the first and third King Edwards, both celebrated as great rulers by the Elizabethan historians. The memory of his warrior father persists throughout the action, standing in latent criticism of his own military incompetence which eventually leads to the *débâcle* of the English defeat at Bannockburn, acidly reported by the Earl of Lancaster in Scene 6. It is telling that he is often described as 'Great Edward Longshanks' issue' (11. 12) rather than as an Edward in his own right: the dead King still keeps him in minority. Even more strikingly, so does his successor: in Scene 18, Prince Edward is appointed viceroy, a position usually held by a Lord Protector acting on behalf of an under-age monarch; and in his straightforward loyalty to the crown, even in difficult circumstances, the young prince is indeed his father's senior in political maturity.

[20] Howard Goorney, *The Theatre Workshop Story* (London, 1981), p. 193.
[21] Simon Russell Beale, quoted by Matt Wolf, 'A Fop is Crowned', *The Times*, 7 July 1990.

King Edward (Simon Russell Beale) kneels to Gaveston (Grant Thatcher) in the 1990 RSC production (photo: Michael Le Poer Trench)

The most important figure to overshadow Edward, however, is Gaveston. Portrayed as the more balanced, the more intelligent, and the more astute of the two men, Gaveston is clearly the dominant partner: it is suggestive that Mortimer Junior should grumble that he wears in his cap 'A jewel of more value than the crown' (4. 416), outdoing Edward even in headgear. In the first scene he is

unashamedly candid about how the relationship can be manipulat-
ed to his own political advantage: an erotic show, for instance, will
serve not only for entertainment but also to 'draw the pliant King
which way I please' (1. 52). This can be seen as dangerous cyni-
cism, in contrast with the innocence of Edward's uncomplicated
love; but it is also an aspect of the skilful, pragmatic *savoir faire* that
is far more attractive to an audience than Edward's tiresomely
childish behaviour.

Such a response is compounded by Gaveston's distinctive mode
of expression. Marlowe never wrote drabber verse than that spoken
by most of the people in *Edward the Second*, but Gaveston alone can
rise to the evocative, aesthetic sensuousness most associated with
the dramatist:

> Like sylvan nymphs my pages shall be clad,
> My men like satyrs grazing on the lawns
> Shall with their goat-feet dance an antic hay;
> Sometime a lovely boy in Dian's shape,
> With hair that gilds the water as it glides,
> Crownets of pearl about his naked arms,
> And in his sportful hands an olive tree
> To hide those parts which men delight to see   (1. 57–64)

Relieving the stark, plain, regular dialogue so common in this play,
such speeches form little islands of beauty amid the harsh, grey re-
alities of politics; and inevitably they affect our attitude to the character who speaks them. It is understandable that readers and
theatregoers have often registered some disappointment with the
play after Gaveston's death.

In Gaveston's appeal lies the challenge of *Edward the Second*. In
part this is because he is attractive for qualities which run counter
to conventional morality: his intelligence and political cunning are
the stuff of amoral Machiavellian *virtù* rather than Christian virtue.
The mere fact of our attraction, moreover, complicates our response to Edward. It is relevant that Gaveston's set-piece speeches
are not only beautiful but openly homoerotic: they offer us a window on the private world which all lovers create for themselves, the
equivalent in the play's verbal text of the 'nook or corner' (4. 72)
of the realm which Edward would reserve from the barons to frolic with his Gaveston. We may not sympathize with the King in the
play's early stages, but we are given a strong incentive to empathize
with his feelings for his lover.

It would be facile, however, to conclude that the play merely
works to induce, by indirections, an appreciation of the experience
of gay sexuality: that would be to underestimate the strength of the
conventional responses which are also evoked. Edward is not only

homosexual but a king, and royal sexuality – of any shade – was a subject surrounded by complexes and phobias in Elizabethan times. During the first half of Elizabeth I's reign, one of the most fervent political hopes was that the Queen would marry and produce an heir to the throne. Without a clear successor to carry on the Tudor dynasty, it was feared that competing candidates for the English crown might brew a civil war like the one that was currently devastating France – a political nightmare that runs through most of the English history plays of the time, including *Edward the Second*. But the Queen never married, and by the 1590s she was well past child-bearing age. English court culture's response was to turn her into an almost mythological figure – constant, unchanging, immortal – and thereby to neutralize through fantasy the fear of an uncertain future. A crucial element of this neurotic wish-fulfilment was that Elizabeth's body had never been sexually penetrated: she was a Virgin Queen. In short, England made a virtue of necessity: the hope that Elizabeth would become sexually active turned perforce into a celebration of the fact that she had not.

For audiences in 1592, then, Marlowe's tragedy of a royal sodomite must have been all very unlike the home life of their own dear Queen: in his sexual incontinence, Edward II stands in stark contrast with Elizabeth I. The contrast is, paradoxically, most acute in that Gaveston's psychological dominance in the relationship evidently reflects a physical dominance. Although the play's lovers are frequently compared with the pederasts of antiquity, Gaveston's initial choice of a heterosexual parallel is more provocative in that it leaves no doubt as to the assignment of roles in the sexual act: when he puts himself in the place of Leander, he leaves the woman's part to Edward. The implication is understated, but clear: it is he who buggers Edward, and not vice versa. Whereas Queen Elizabeth was celebrated for her inviolate body, King Edward's has been penetrated.

This is not a detail which Marlowe found in any of his sources: no previous writer on the subject had dwelt on the precise physical nature of the two men's relationship. The effect of specifying it was to maximize the potential for shock by allying the commonplace moralistic reaction to sodomy with the more particular anxieties associated with the violation of a royal body. The play empowers anti-gay prejudices just as much as it solicits understanding and empathy, so that a sensitive and alert audience would find itself being encouraged to see Gaveston (and by extension his relationship with Edward) in two incompatible ways: he is not only an attractive figure but also a sexual criminal and a traitor. Because both extremes of response are promoted independently, the play resists simplification into a tract on one or the other side of the issue: rather it circumvents both moralistic and liberal preconceptions about its subject-matter. Edward's homosexuality is indeed an essential, unignorable element in the conflict, but the play is not in any straightforward way the 'gay classic' which some modern commentators have wanted it to be.

POLITICS

Gay issues have not always been perceived as central in the play. For much of the twentieth century, *Edward the Second* rode the back of Shakespeare's *King Richard II*: often staged as the rarer half of a double bill, its interest lay in its being an important relative of the better-known play. Accordingly, attention focused on Marlowe's political action of a weak king deposed by his barons, and what one critic called, in perhaps the least successful euphemism ever, the play's 'fundamental offence' was toned down in production to suit the prevailing canons of sexual morality.[22] This is not attributable simply to the prudishness of individual actors and directors: while no longer the hanging matters they had been in the 1590s, all homosexual acts remained criminal in Britain until 1967. More recent productions were able openly to explore the play's gay themes primarily because of the shift in public attitudes to private behaviour which led to the change in the law, and indeed to the abolition of theatre censorship in 1968.

The risk to the play in a modern liberal community is that critics and productions will merely invert the emphasis of earlier generations, and concentrate exclusively on its personal concerns at the expense of its public ones. For example, it is sometimes suggested that pre-1967 productions emphasized Gaveston's foreign origins by way of compensation for their avoidance of his homosexuality: the barons' xenophobia is taken to be merely a polite substitute for homophobia. To concentrate exclusively on the latter, however, is just as limiting as to ignore it. The play makes much of the fact that Gaveston is a Frenchman with overtly foreign tastes: he diverts the King with 'Italian masques' (1. 54), and wears Continental fashions such as his 'short Italian hooded cloak' (4. 414) and his 'Tuscan cap' (415); the clothes and their overseas origins are detailed with an almost obsessive precision by Mortimer Junior. For the play's original audience, the point could be taken further: sodomy, another penchant of Gaveston's, was also thought to be a particular predilection of the Italians.[23] Accordingly, xenophobia and homophobia were not entirely distinct attitudes: Gaveston is a contaminating Continental influence that has infiltrated the body

---

[22] J. M. Robertson, *Marlowe: A Conspectus* (London, 1931), p. 33.
[23] Alan Bray, *Homosexuality in Renaissance England* (London, 1982), p. 75.

of the nation, but he has also infiltrated the body of its King. Political and personal issues are a continuum – and from the barons' point of view, that is the problem.

Mortimer Junior expresses the objections to Gaveston in an important expository speech:

> Uncle, his wanton humour grieves not me,
> But this I scorn, that one so basely born
> Should by his sovereign's favour grow so pert,
> And riot it with the treasure of the realm
> While soldiers mutiny for want of pay.
> He wears a lord's revènue on his back,
> And Midas-like he jets it in the court
> With base outlandish cullions at his heels,
> Whose proud fantastic liveries make such show
> As if that Proteus, god of shapes, appeared
> I have not seen a dapper jack so brisk;
> He wears a short Italian hooded cloak,
> Larded with pearl; and in his Tuscan cap
> A jewel of more value than the crown.
> Whiles other walk below, the King and he
> From out a window laugh at such as we,
> And flout our train and jest at our attire.
> Uncle, 'tis this that makes me impatient.   (4. 403-20)

The case is complex and remarkably distinct from the Elizabethan moralists' theologically-derived attitude to gay sexuality. Edward's 'wanton humour' (403) is not the central problem: Mortimer Senior has already made a strong argument for tolerating the King's liking for catamites. Homosexuality is not considered intrinsically unnatural: 'The mightiest kings have had their minions' (392), he points out, and cites five classical precedents to prove it. The barons can afford to put up with this, he suggests, because the lovers constitute no serious political threat: Edward is 'mild and calm' (389) by nature, Gaveston 'vain' and 'light-headed' (401). The conservative preference for clear lines of demarcation enables him to draw an implicit boundary between the King's public actions and his private tastes; but it also enables his nephew to complain of the persistent infraction of that boundary.

Edward's relationship with Gaveston is dangerous to the barons because it is not furtive: the objection is not that the King is gay, but that he's glad to be gay. At one level, the flaunting of his preferences is culturally threatening because it disrupts the traditional ways in which value is measured and expressed. Effeminacy rules, for example, in a court where taste in clothes is considered more important than such manly pursuits as warfare. If clear distinctions, with an implicit hierarchy of merit, are central to the Mortimers' thinking, Edward promotes transgression and inversion: ennobled peasants, foreigners in England, womanish men. Less subjectively, however, there is also the broader issue of political priorities and public maladministration. Gaveston's wardrobe is worth 'a lord's revenue' (4. 408), and it is paid for from 'the treasure of the realm' (406) which should be spent on a higher defence budget: England is, after all, at war with its territorial neighbour, Scotland.

From the start of the play it is clear that Edward has little sense of the distinction between private friendship and official patronage: Gaveston is invited to 'share the kingdom with thy dearest friend' (1. 2), as if it were a personal possession to be distributed at will. Accordingly, the King's private wishes are treated as if they are matters of crown policy, in competition with all the other demands on the public purse. Part of the problem is the immature excess of Edward's feelings: they call for a material expression which outstrips both financial and political prudence. There is some justice in Mortimer Junior's pointed accusation,

> The idle triumphs, masques, lascivious shows,
> And prodigal gifts bestowed on Gaveston
> Have drawn thy treasure dry and made thee weak;
> The murmuring commons overstretchèd hath.　　(6. 154–7)

As well as eating into his own reserves of capital, Edward has shifted the fiscal burden, in two ways: he has increased direct taxation of the commons, but he has also reduced the crown's responsibilities – for example by requiring Mortimer to pay his uncle's ransom, even though the old man was taken prisoner fighting for the King. In effect, Edward has simultaneously fostered discontent among his subjects and reduced his resources for suppressing that discontent.

What makes matters worse from the barons' point of view is that Edward showers his boyfriend not only with material gifts but also with public offices. It may be that Gaveston loves him 'more than all the world' (4. 77), but there is a sense in which, for Gaveston, Edward *is*, if not the world, then at least the kingdom: it is through the King that he becomes, in rapid succession, Lord High Chamberlain, Chief Secretary to the State and the King, Earl of Cornwall, King and Lord of the Isle of Man, and Bishop of Coventry. This is disruptive, not just because it introduces a new and influential nobleman to the political scene, but because it undermines the hereditary principle which is the foundation of the aristocracy's claim to power. A subject to which the barons repeatedly return is Gaveston's social origins: Edward's minion is a *villein*, a peasant of lowly rank, 'made an earl' (2. 11) through royal decree alone. If noblemen can be made as well as born – and Gaveston is only the first – then aristocratic titles cease to be inherently meaningful.

Even before his elevation to the peerage, Gaveston's relationship with Edward effectively bypasses the old aristocracy:

What greater bliss can hap to Gaveston,
Than live and be the favourite of a king?
. . .
Farewell, base stooping to the lordly peers;
My knee shall bow to none but to the King. (1. 4–19)

At one level this is again a matter of affront to traditional hierarchy: 'basely born' Gaveston will accept only one man as his social and political superior. More broadly, it also indicates the emergence of new criteria for empowerment. The King's homosexuality means that his lovers can be directly active in the affairs of state in a way that, in this culture, women cannot; and his political naïvety makes him all too ready to distribute royal favour (and therefore power) according to sexual attractiveness rather than noble birth. Aristocratic titles are therefore sidelined, as Gaveston's successor in Edward's affections, Spencer Junior, recognizes:

No greater titles happen unto me
Than to be favoured of your majesty. (6. 251–2)

The offices and earldoms which Edward distributes to his minions and their associates are merely the outward expression of his love and support; but it is that personal nexus with the King which counts, and not the earldoms themselves. The effect is to shift the balance of power away from the hereditary barons, something which, in practice, the impoverished Edward has neither the resources nor the strength of character to sustain. Unavoidably, the result is civil war in England.

In short, then, *Edward the Second* portrays the King's sexuality as a causal factor in a large-scale political disaster. A number of problems, of structure and of characterization, arise when the play is treated as being predominantly personal rather than public in its concerns. For example, actors, accustomed to taking their characters on a linear 'journey', are sometimes perplexed by the discontinuous way in which they behave: the Queen turns from loyal, abused wife to scheming adulteress, for example, and Mortimer Junior from aristocratic little-Englander to Machiavellian power-seeker. Lord Maltravers undergoes such a transformation, from the King's faithful ally to an accessory in his murder, that for nearly 150 years the play's editors mistook him for two separate roles.[24] These characters don't change according to internal factors which might provide a clear through-line of psychological development:

---

[24] See the Note on the Text, pp. xl–xli.

they are subordinate to the shifting dispositions of power in the broader progression of the action, and their personal inconsistencies arise as they accommodate themselves to the prevailing political circumstances.

In this connection, the most revealing political confrontation in the play's early stages is also the most low-key, when the Mortimers are left alone on stage at the end of Scene 4, and the uncle tries unsuccessfully to persuade his nephew to condone Edward's relationship with Gaveston. This is probably better understood as a pragmatic rather than a genuinely liberal position: at this point the King is still the undisputed centre of power, so it is politically prudent to humour him where possible. That is why loyalty is initially the Queen's safest course. Such political quietism goes unrewarded, however: Isabella merely prolongs her distressing situation as a female cuckold, and Mortimer Senior is left a prisoner of war in Scotland after Edward refuses to pay his ransom. The active opposition advocated by Mortimer Junior wins the argument, and so *de facto* power slips away from the King, and with it go most of his allies: Mortimer fills the power vacuum created when Edward is defeated and imprisoned, and the Queen and Maltravers gravitate towards him. In effect, these are figures defined more by their relationship to power than by any conventional, personal concept of linear characterization.

Recognizing that the political struggle is paramount also helps to account for the apparently meandering and directionless quality of parts of the action. For example, the developments of the first half-hour seem merely to cancel each other out, with Gaveston first recalled from exile in France, then banished to Ireland, and then recalled from Ireland: the narrative resembles a see-saw, hoisting Gaveston up and down in repetitive series, but going nowhere. The disappearance of the charismatic minion half-way through, executed by the barons after Scene 10, can also make the play seem broken-backed, the middle sections lost in the convolutions of civil war before the action regains its focus and direction at the end. Critics are apt to apologize for Marlowe, treating these features as structural weaknesses which must be explained away as an unfortunate side-effect of compressing the twenty-one years of Edward's reign (1307–27) into a single play; but it is as likely to be a deliberate technique for representing an escalating power struggle, which Marlowe perhaps learned from the similar back-and-forth plotting of Shakespeare's civil war play, *Henry VI, Part 3* (1591).

The problem is that an audience's personal engagement with Gaveston can all too easily pull focus from the developing political conflict. To a degree this is a result of an unevenness in Marlowe's imaginative writing, which is most powerful at the beginning and end when most engaged with the personal aspect of Edward's ex-

Simon Russell Beale as King Edward in the 1990 RSC production (photo: Michael Le Poer Trench)

periences. It is also the case, however, that the characters, barons as well as King, are excessively fixated on Gaveston in the early scenes: 'If you love us,' Mortimer Senior tells Edward, 'hate Gaveston' (1. 79). Yet Gaveston is far from being the central character: 'what's extraordinary is that it's not principally about a homosexual relationship,' comments Simon Russell Beale; 'Edward's greatest relationship is with his crown.'[25] This means that the treat-

[25] Simon Russell Beale, quoted by Matt Wolf, 'A Fop is Crowned'.

ment of Gaveston in performance is of primary importance in the negotiation which any producer must undertake between the play's personal and political dimensions. If he is not an attractive figure, then we lose sympathy and understanding for Edward's fascination with him; the conflict becomes one-sided, the play just the story of an inadequate King's unseating. But if Gaveston is made too attractive, then we are liable to fall under his spell. In other words, he must be both charismatic and transparent, both a desired person and a bargaining counter: he must be an element in our sense of the clash between monarch and nobility, but he must not dominate it. Removing Gaveston doesn't end the war because ultimately Gaveston is only a symptom, and can be replaced with Spencer Junior; the point at issue, which the minions can occlude, is the way Edward uses the power of his office for private ends.

To sum up, the play's overall unity lies in its political action; but it also requires its audience to shift focus from private to public and back. In the modern theatre, one of the key determinants of the balance between the two is the scenic design: the look of a production defines whether it is set in a realistic England or a subjective landscape of the mind. In 1956, for example, the Theatre Workshop production took place on a raked stage covered with a huge map of England, starkly emphasizing not only the site of the struggle but the prize. In contrast, more recent productions, with their sympathetic emphasis on Edward's sexual escapism, have tended to create a visual impression of an ugly England scarcely worth fighting for: in 1969, the setting was 'a slippery looking circle like a spreading oil slick' with 'sickly greens and dead reds'; the 1986 cast had to cope with 'a pit of peat with a stanchion tap on its perimeter, coldly dripping water to make enough mud for an entire grovel of courtiers to splatter through'; and in 1990 the Swan stage became a rubbish tip, with Mortimer Junior's second-half costume turning him into a giant parasite fly.[26] In these cases, clearly, the stress was more or less against any sense of an objective reality.

In this aspect, the 1947 BBC production is particularly interesting, if only by default rather than design. The director, Stephen Harrison, was especially concerned to establish a sense of period authenticity: all the props and costumes were 'to look as nearly as possible early 14th century', David Markham's make-up as Edward was based on the image of the King on his tomb in Gloucester Cathedral, and Harrison even issued the actors of Gaveston, Spencer Junior, and Lancaster with extracts from a 'standard history of the period' on the character of the historical originals.[27]

---

[26] Nancy Banks-Smith, *The Guardian*, 8 August 1970; David Roper, *Plays and Players*, December 1986, 25.

[27] Caversham: BBC Written Archives Centre, T5/164. All details about the production derive from this file, unless otherwise stated.

However, the designer, Barry Learoyd, despaired of representing the play's multiple locations within the conventions of television naturalism, and set the action against 'Penumbrascope screens' which gave a suggestion of place through shadow effects, with on-screen captions to identify the settings more precisely.[28] The result must have been a striking juxtaposition of realistic foreground and abstract, surrealistic backdrop; and this is especially notable in that it echoes the text's own ambiguous treatment of its setting.

Large-scale movable scenery was not part of the theatrical technology available in the 1590s: plays created their fictional locations through language and the foreground visuals of actors' costumes and groupings on stage. Elizabethan history plays in particular are often concerned with the English geography against which their great events take place, not unlike Western films fetishizing the landscape of America. What is distinctive about Marlowe's play is that England as a setting has both real and allegorical qualities: the action ranges across the length of the nation, from London to Tynemouth, but at times it also occupies, simultaneously, a country of the mind. This is particularly the case in the later stages as Edward's destruction approaches. For example, the castle where the prisoner-King is first taken is not only Kenilworth but, in the original spelling, 'Killingworth', and the Mower who betrays him is also the figure of Death with his scythe. Both the verbal and the visual pun help to telegraph Edward's impending fate. More broadly, too, they introduce a vein of fantastic subjectivity as the narrative draws back inwards to the private dimension of Edward's tragedy. After a predominantly political central movement, the play ends as it began, in the King's personal space.

CRUELTY

'None shall know which way he died,' promises Lightborne (23. 24); but *everyone* knows. The terrible death of King Edward II is notorious, in history as in the play. Holinshed describes it explicitly:

> [Maltravers and Gourney] came suddenly one night into the chamber where he lay in bed fast asleep, and with heavy featherbeds or a table (as some write) being cast upon him, they kept him down and withal put into his fundament an horn, and through the same they thrust up into his body an hot spit, or (as other have) through the pipe of a trumpet a plumber's instrument of iron made very hot, the which passing up into his entrails, and being rolled to and fro, burnt the same, but so as no appearance of any wound or hurt outwardly might be once perceived. His cry did move many within the castle and town

[28] *Radio Times*, 24 October 1947, 29.

of Berkeley to compassion, plainly hearing him utter a wailful noise, as the tormentors were about to murder him, so that divers being awakened therewith . . . prayed heartily to God to receive his soul, when they understood by his cry what the matter meant.[29]

For many years editors and directors alike did their best to cover up the grisly details. The stage history offers a catalogue of evasion and misrepresentation. William Poel had the murder done behind a traverse curtain at the back of the stage, from which Maltravers, Gourney, and Lightborne re-emerged after the King's dying scream. Fifty-three years later, Joan Littlewood brought the dirty business onto the stage, but only underneath a cloak thrown across Edward's body: 'only his face was seen . . . and as the red-hot iron was supposed to enter his bowels the music gave a terrifying shriek'.[30] Daringly for 1947, Stephen Harrison's television version showed the murder, but the spit was not seen on screen (or indeed present in the studio), and the victim was obscured under a large mattress. Frank Benson was able to go further in his 1905 production only by having Edward killed on stage by smothering rather than anal penetration, presumably without the scream mentioned in the text.[31]

There has been a similar pattern of genteel obscurantism in editions of the play. The original quarto gives no stage direction describing the killing, and its earliest editors in the eighteenth and nineteenth centuries did not feel inclined to supply one. When Alexander Dyce did so in his edition of 1850, it was entirely misleading: 'KING EDWARD *is murdered by holding him down on the bed with the table, and stamping on it*' – not a method likely to fulfil Lightborne's promise of secrecy.[32] Astonishingly, Dyce's stage direction was very popular with his successors, and could still be found in print as late as 1979. Most twentieth-century editors, however, have preferred the simpler opacity of *'King Edward is murdered'*, without actually saying how.

On stage, the scene has become more graphic as productions have grown more open about the play's homosexual themes: Ian McKellen's Edward was spitted in full view of the audience in 1969, and in 1990 Simon Russell Beale's was hoisted upside-down, filthy and naked, while a thick, red-hot, smoking iron was forced downwards into his bowels. The earlier tendency to suppress this

[29] Raphael Holinshed, *Chronicles of England, Scotland, and Ireland*, 2nd ed. (London, 1587), vol. 3, p. 341.

[30] Joan Littlewood, *Joan's Book* (London, 1994), p. 467.

[31] *The Stage*, 4 May 1905; cf. *Stratford-upon-Avon Herald*, 5 May 1905.

[32] *The Works of Christopher Marlowe*, ed. Alexander Dyce (London, 1850), vol. 2, p. 284.

sort of thing was more than simple squeamishness, however: neither Poel nor Harrison shrank from including Mortimer Junior's severed head in the final scene, and in Benson's production it even dripped blood onto the stage, to the distress of some ladies in the audience.[33] There is something uniquely horrible about Edward's murder, probably the most gruesome in the entire corpus of Elizabethan drama – and Elizabethan drama is not noted for its restraint in the portrayal of violent death. Recent productions may have been more explicit, but the self-protective impulse still remains strong, even if today we are more likely to insulate ourselves with off-colour laughter ('They don't like it up 'em!') than by tampering with the text.

It is possible to argue that a more restrained treatment of the murder can be effective: there is an understated horror in details such as, in Poel's version, Lightborne pulling on his gloves as he returned to the stage.[34] Unfortunately, such an approach disrupts the wider balance of the play, in which physical cruelty, both imagined and enacted, is a major element. There is a savage streak throughout which is first apparent in the entertainment which Gaveston plans for the King: an enactment of the death of Actaeon, transformed into a stag and torn to pieces by his own hounds. There is a sense of voyeurism, of Edward luxuriating in images of cruelty: 'Such things as these best please his majesty' (1. 70). When crossed, moreover, he is prone to indulge in sadistic arias showing an imaginative engagement with violence which outstrips his power to inflict it: on hearing that Gaveston has been murdered, for instance, he threatens,

> I will have heads and lives for him as many
> As I have manors, castles, towns, and towers.
> Treacherous Warwick! Traitorous Mortimer!
> If I be England's king, in lakes of gore
> Your headless trunks, your bodies will I trail,
> That you may drink your fill and quaff in blood   (11. 132–7)

Such spectacles are, of course, the antithesis of his own voluptuous desires. The overall structure of the action takes him across that antithesis in a kind of sado-masochistic arc, from the pursuit of extremes of sensual gratification to the experience of extremes of bodily pain.

As with the play's concern with homosexuality, it is possible for critics to assume that this recurrent emphasis on physical cruelty is

---

[33] *The Stage*, 4 May 1905. The detail was cut from the second of the two performances.

[34] Robert Speaight, *William Poel and the Elizabethan Revival* (Cambridge, Mass., 1954), pp. 179–80.

a direct reflection of a documented aspect of its author's personal character: after Marlowe's death, his acquaintance Thomas Kyd wrote that he was 'intemperate and of a cruel heart'.[35] To privilege the obsessive over the artistic like this, however, is reductive: the play's atrocities and humiliations are not just indulged for themselves, but are part of the formal patterning of the overall action. For example, the forcible shaving of Edward's beard by his keepers Maltravers and Gourney in Scene 22 has its own rationale and effectiveness, but also wider connotations. A deposed but living king is a potential focus of dissent, illustrated by the fate of the Earl of Kent soon afterwards: Edward must be made to disappear from the political scene, and in the short term one way of achieving this is to change his face so that he will not be recognized. (A more permanent solution comes soon afterwards, of course.) What is most disturbing about the incident is its excess: it is not only an intrusion on Edward's personal dignity but also physically unpleasant in the barbers' use of effluent, 'channel water' (22. 27), to wash him. When Edward calls on 'Immortal powers' (37) to help him against 'these daring men, / That wrongs their liege and sovereign, England's King' (39–40), however, he is ineffectual not least because of his own former misbehaviour towards those powers' earthly representative, when he and Gaveston assaulted the Bishop of Coventry and rolled him in the gutter:

> Throw off his golden mitre, rend his stole,
> And in the channel christen him anew.   (1. 186–7)

Channel water for the Bishop, channel water for the King: Edward's disregard for others' dignity and high office during his ascendancy cuts the other way in his captivity. His complaint throughout is that, as King, he is entitled to better treatment: 'They give me bread and water, being a king' (24. 61). But if high birth and hereditary titles do not matter, then this must be as true of himself, born to wear the crown, as of the barons he has disregarded.

Edward's death is the ultimate example of this kind of parallel patterning. In a sense, the assassin Lightborne is a terrible *alter ego* of Gaveston; some productions even double the parts. He too is an Italianate figure, but what he has brought back from the Mediterranean is not masques and fashions, but the art of murder:

> I learned in Naples how to poison flowers,
> To strangle with a lawn thrust through the throat,
> To pierce the windpipe with a needle's point,
> Or, whilst one is asleep, to take a quill

---

[35] Thomas Kyd, *The Works*, ed. F. S. Boas (Oxford, 1901), p. cix.

And blow a little powder in his ears,
Or open his mouth and pour quicksilver down.   (23. 30–5)

Though sadistic rather than homosexual, the language here, with
its quasi-erotic attention to physical detail, has the same voluptuous
qualities as Gaveston's. Moreover, Lightborne is the only character
to show tenderness to the imprisoned Edward; playing the assassin
in the 1969 Prospect production, Robert Eddison treated it explicitly as a homoerotic encounter, picking up on the latent implications of his offering the King a bed. Finally, of course, the
murder itself recalls the most physically intimate aspect of the relationship with Gaveston: it is a form of symbolic buggery, repel-
lent, yet also grotesquely apt.

In effect, then, the events of the closing stages are patterned to
suggest the process of 'tit for tat' implicit in the Golden Rule of
Christian teaching: 'whatsoever ye would that men should do to
you, even so do ye to them'.[36] The retributive implications are re-
inforced by the symbolic landscape into which the play has moved.
Although the action is firmly secular, with no hint of direct inter-
vention by any supernatural or divine force, the allegorical under-
currents create a metaphysical dimension: if Edward is betrayed by
the figure of Death, then in his imprisonment he is sent to Hell. His
dungeon, probably situated under the stage, is 'the sink / Wherein
the filth of all the castle falls' (24. 55–6), aptly called by Maltravers
'the lake' (25); but 'the lake' was also a term associated with the pit
of Hell. Lightborne adds to the effect: it was often said in the sixteenth century that an Englishman Italianate is a devil incarnate,
and this one is even named after Lucifer.[37] All this encourages us
to interpret Edward's death in terms of the torments of the
damned. In the patristic theologian Tertullian's influential conception of Hell, sinners were punished in kind. Marlowe's former collaborator Thomas Nashe imagined it vividly:

> he that all his lifetime was a great fornicator, hath all the diseases of lust con-
> tinually hanging upon him, and is constrained, the more to augment his mis-
> ery, to have congress every hour with hags and old witches; and he that was a
> great drunkard here on earth, hath his penance assigned him, to carouse him-
> self drunk with dish-wash and vinegar, and surfeit four times a day with sour
> ale and small beer. As so of the rest, as the usurer to swallow molten gold, the
> glutton to eat nothing but toads, and the murderer to be still stabbed with
> daggers, but never die.[38]

What more appropriate for the sodomite than to be spitted through
the anus in an appalling parody of his sinful bodily pleasures?

---

[36] Matthew 7:12 (Geneva translation).
[37] The English 'light-borne' is a direct translation of the Latin 'lucifer'.
[38] Thomas Nashe, *Pierce Penniless*, in *The Works*, vol. 1, p. 218.

The final movement has, then, a built-in inducement to read the action in an orthodox, moralizing way, and conclude that the homosexual King gets his just deserts: the 1590s nightmare of the violated royal body returns to the play in a hideously perverted form. This would not be a surprising interpretation in Elizabethan England, when brutal punishments were institutionalized for criminals in this world and sinners in the next. But is this what we actually feel when we see the play enacted? It is often suggested that sixteenth-century playgoers were hardened to violence by the experience of public executions, but in fact there is evidence that people wept with human sympathy for the victim. There is reason to think that Edward's death would have elicited the same reaction.

The murder is easiest to perform with Edward's head downstage. As with all theatrical violence, the paramount concern is not to injure the actor, and this means masking the actual point of penetration. Some courageous modern actors have gone further, including Ian McKellen and Simon Russell Beale, but in doing so risked blunting the effect with the distraction of nudity: 'I don't think he can be naked for too much of the scene,' remarked Beale, 'because I'm sure people would be more interested in my willie and not listening to the words I'm saying.'[39] The text does not require this ultimate humiliation: Edward is covered as he dies, in that he is pinned down with a table and a featherbed, the latter cushioning the pressure so that, as Lightborne directs, there will be no tell-tale bruises on the body. With the audience on three sides of the stage, the usual arrangement of an Elizabethan open-air theatre, the sightlines would have required Edward's lower half to be upstage. This means that much of the impact must come from the actor's facial and vocal performance: we can see clearly what Lightborne is doing, but the focus is on a human face contorted in indescribable pain, and a scream that is loud enough, Maltravers fears, to wake the town. Can you still argue that the punishment fits the crime?

The murder must be staged, then, precisely because it is obscene: the unspeakable physical reality is part of the effect. If it is politely left to the audience's imagination, it can all too easily be rationalized as talion punishment; but, as with its treatment of homosexuality, the play is more complex and disturbing than this. It *contains* the orthodox view on the touchy subjects it addresses, with a degree of conviction that undoubtedly satisfied the Elizabethan censor, but any sensitive audience will see other dimensions too. The point is not that sympathy and judgement will somehow qualify one another, though this may be the eventual outcome as individual playgoers think it through: the drama works not to make a compromise for its audience, but simply to compromise them, to

---

[39] Simon Russell Beale, quoted by Terence Michael Stephenson, 'Sweet Lies'.

give them an emotional commitment to both points of view. This is what makes it such an uncomfortable, challenging play: its persistent attention to both sides of the issue – gay and homophobic, public and private, moralistic and liberal. That is no doubt why so many of its interpreters – actors and directors, editors and critics and teachers – have tried so hard to reduce it to rule. Whatever you do with this edition, please try to resist that temptation.

NOTE ON THE TEXT

The control-text for this edition is the 1594 octavo, the earliest and only authoritative edition of *Edward the Second*, which was probably printed from an authorial manuscript. It is a particularly rare book: only one copy survives, and is held by the Zentralbibliothek, Zürich, Switzerland; a second copy, incorporating some uncorrected formes, was in existence in the Landesbibliothek, Cassel, Germany, until it was destroyed by bombing during the Second World War. Although the edition was printed in octavo format, it has the general appearance of a quarto, and the editors have adopted the traditional practice of referring to it as Q.

Subsequent editions were printed in 1598, 1612, and 1622 (Q2–4 respectively), but these are of limited interest: in each case the compositors sought to improve the punctuation and spelling of Q, as well as introducing a number of their own inauthoritative readings. There are also a number of peculiar and unlikely variants in a manuscript version of the first seventy lines of the play, in the Dyce collection at the Victoria and Albert Museum, London. Produced to replace the first two leaves of a quarto, this is dated 1593, and so purports to be the earliest surviving text of *Edward the Second*. Recent scholarship, however, has shown that the manuscript was probably prepared by a scribe copying from Q.

Q presents the editor with a number of technical problems: stage directions are often missing or wrongly positioned, speech prefixes are inconsistent, and there are a number of compositorial bungles. In this edition, the punctuation has been silently altered where necessary and speech prefixes have been regularized. All significant changes to the lineation of verse are recorded in the notes; however, changes to the division of prose passages and verse lines split to accommodate them within the physical dimensions of Q are not recorded. The spelling has been modernized throughout according to the principles set down by Stanley Wells in his *Modernizing Shakespeare's Spelling* (Oxford, 1979); a few interesting cases where the old form differs significantly from the modern are recorded in the notes. Proper names have also been silently modernized, so that, for example, 'Matrevis' becomes Maltravers, 'Gurney' becomes Gourney, and 'Bartley' becomes Berkeley.

One such modernization, of 'Killingworth' to Kenilworth, raises difficult issues. As discussed in the Introduction, the name can be taken to combine geographical precision with an undertone foreshadowing Edward's eventual fate. This means that the modernizing editor is faced with two options, neither of which preserves the

full original effect. Each, moreover, has particular disadvantages of
its own: to retain 'Killingworth' in an otherwise fully modernized
edition is implicitly, and erroneously, to move the location several
hundred miles, to the castleless Tyneside village now famous for its
associations with George Stephenson; while the name of
Kenilworth has picked up irrelevant romantic connotations from
Sir Walter Scott's novel of that title (1821). Besides consistency
with the editors' practice elsewhere in the edition, the case for modernization turns on the primacy of the geographical reference,
whereas the suggestion of killing is only a *potential* pun, a secondary
meaning probably, but not necessarily, intended by the author.[1]
The spelling 'Killingworth' is simply the form of the name used by
Holinshed and retained by Marlowe: there is no positive evidence
that he deliberately adopted it for literary effect. In point of fact, no
killing takes place at 'Killingworth': Edward is moved to Berkeley
before he is murdered (21. 60). It is not, then, an ironic name for
Edward's final destination, like the King's Jerusalem chamber in
Shakespeare's *Henry IV, Part 2*. Moreover, there is no point at
which the characters seem aware that 'Killingworth' is anything
other than a place name. While the editors believe that a secondary
meaning is present, creating for the audience a generalized ominous
effect, this remains a matter of critical inference rather than demon-
strable textual fact. Accordingly, the modernized form 'Kenilworth'
is adopted in this edition.

In the treatment of stage directions, the editors have been concerned to balance fidelity to the written text with the need to convey to a reader something of the experience of seeing the play in the
theatre. Q's Latin directions have been silently translated, with the
exception of *'Exit'* and *'Exeunt'*, and square brackets have been
used to denote directions (or parts thereof) supplied by the editors.
A number of directions to enter are given late in Q, presumably to
indicate the point at which the characters concerned enter the action, rather than the stage; the editors have repositioned such directions to indicate the point at which those characters become
visible to a theatre audience, and sometimes to other characters already on stage.

There are numerous inconsistencies in the designation of char-
acters in stage directions and speech prefixes: Edward is also
'King', Isabella is also 'Queen', Kent is also 'Edmund', and so on.
The most textually important of these inconsistencies concerns
Maltravers, who is first introduced as the Earl of Arundel in Scene
9, but who is most frequently referred to as 'Matrevis', even in the

---

[1] Cf. Stanley Wells, *Modernizing Shakespeare's Spelling* (Oxford, 1979), pp. 10–12.

dialogue. Since Arundel and Maltravers were distinct historical persons, editors have usually supposed these references in Scenes 9, 11, and 16 to be erroneous, and have treated 'Arundel' as a separate character from 'Matrevis' who appears in Scenes 21, 22, 24, and 25; the error was explained by the hypothesis that Marlowe had intended the two roles to be doubled, and had confused their names accordingly. This edition, however, presupposes that there is no textual error and that Q's 'Arundel' and 'Matrevis' are simply variant ways of designating a single character. Marlowe was probably influenced by the fact that the later Earls of Arundel also held the title Lord Maltravers; it was not the only occasion on which his treatment of the fourteenth-century barons was affected by the heraldry of his own time.[2]

Q contains no act- or scene-divisions. In 1818, James Broughton introduced a five-act structure which has been adopted (with some variations) in most subsequent editions.[3] Such a structure was recognized in Marlowe's time as a literary device, and some plays (including *The Comedy of Errors* and *Henry V*) were written in five acts. There is no evidence that this was the case with *Edward the Second*, however. Moreover, until 1608 at the earliest, act-divisions were not used in the open-air theatres for which *Edward the Second* was written: plays were performed continuously from the first scene to the last. The editors have, accordingly, chosen to divide the play only into its scenes, the better to represent its original impact in the theatre.

Although this edition departs from the editorial tradition in several significant respects, the editors' debt to their predecessors remains substantial. The play's first named editor was Robert Dodsley, who included it in his multi-volume collection of *Old Plays* in 1744. The nineteenth century saw the evolution of interventionist editing, and some of the principal textual hypotheses, still accepted by recent editors, were tentatively formulated by Alexander Dyce in 1850 (in *The Works of Christopher Marlowe*, volume 2). In the twentieth century the most important bibliographical work was done in the editions of W. W. Greg (1926) and Fredson Bowers (1973; in *The Complete Works of Christopher Marlowe*, volume 2), while those of H. B. Charlton and R. D. Waller (1933), Charles R. Forker (1994), and Richard Rowland (1994) made especially significant contributions to the play's criti-

---

2 See 13. 25n. The hypothesis is presented at greater length in Martin Wiggins, 'Arundel and Maltravers: A Textual Problem in *Edward II*', *N&Q*, 242 (1997), pp. 42–7.
3 The commonest division of the play is as follows: Scenes 1–4 = Act 1; Scenes 5–9 = Act 2; Scenes 10–13 = Act 3; Scenes 14–19 = Act 4; Scenes 20–25 = Act 5.

cism and exegesis. The editors have also found useful the editions of William Dinsmore Briggs (1914), W. Moelwyn Merchant (1967), Roma Gill (1967), and David Bevington and Eric Rasmussen (1995; in *Doctor Faustus and Other Plays*).

FURTHER READING

Belsey, Catherine, 'Desire's Excess and the English Renaissance Theatre: *Edward II, Troilus and Cressida, Othello*', in Susan Zimmerman (ed.), *Erotic Politics: Desire on the Renaissance Stage* (New York and London, 1992), 84–102

Bevington, David M., *From 'Mankind' to Marlowe: Growth of Structure in the Popular Drama of Tudor England* (Cambridge, Mass., 1962)

Biggs, Murray, 'Some Problems of Acting *Edward II*', in Murray Biggs, Philip Edwards, Inga-Stina Ewbank, and Eugene M. Waith (eds), *The Arts of Performance in Elizabethan and Early Stuart Drama* (Edinburgh, 1991), 192–9

Cole, Douglas, *Suffering and Evil in the Plays of Christopher Marlowe* (Princeton, 1962)

Downie, J. A. and Parnell, J.T. (eds.), *Constructing Christopher Marlowe* (Cambridge, 2000)

Friedenreich, Kenneth, Gill, Roma, and Kuriyama, Constance B. (eds), *'A Poet and a Filthy Play-Maker': New Essays on Christopher Marlowe* (New York, 1988)

Geckle, George L., *'Tamburlaine' and 'Edward II': Text and Performance* (Basingstoke and London, 1988)

Greenblatt, Stephen, *Renaissance Self-Fashioning: From More to Shakespeare* (Chicago and London, 1980)

Hattaway, Michael, *Elizabethan Popular Theatre: Plays in Performance* (London, 1982)

Kelsall, Malcolm, *Christopher Marlowe* (Leiden, 1981)

Kuriyama, Constance Brown, *Christopher Marlow: A Renaissance Life* (Ithaca and London, 2002)

Leech, Clifford, *Christopher Marlowe: Poet for the Stage* (New York, 1986)

Levin, Harry, *The Overreacher: A Study of Christopher Marlowe* (London, 1954)

Lunney, Ruth, *Marlowe and the Popular Tradition: Innovation in the English Drama Before 1595* (Manchester and New York, 2002)

MacLure, Millar (ed.), *Marlowe: The Critical Heritage, 1588–1896* (London, Boston, and Henley, 1979)

McCloskey, Susan, 'The Worlds of *Edward II*', *Renaissance Drama* n.s. 16 (1985), 35–48

Ribner, Irving, 'Marlowe's *Edward II* and the Tudor History Play', *English Literary History* 22 (1955), 243–53

Sanders, Wilbur, *The Dramatist and the Received Idea: Studies in the Plays of Marlowe and Shakespeare* (Cambridge, 1968)

Smith, Bruce R., *Homosexual Desire in Shakespeare's England* (Chicago, 1991)

Thomas, Vivien and Tydeman, William (eds), *Christopher Marlowe: The Plays and their Sources* (London and New York, 1994)

Thurn, David H., 'Sovereignty, Disorder and Fetishism in Marlowe's *Edward II*', *Renaissance Drama* n.s. 21 (1990), 115–41

Weil, Judith, *Christopher Marlowe: Merlin's Prophet* (Cambridge, 1977)

Information about recent productions, including photographs, is available in a variety of locations scattered across the internet. Readers need to bear in mind that websites are not always reliable sources of scholarly information, and that they are often transient; currently available sites can be found using most standard search engines.

(opposite) Title page of the first edition of *Edward the Second*, 1594 (photo: Zentralbibliothek, Zürich)

The troublesome

raigne and lamentable death of
Edward *the second*, *King of*
England: with the tragicall
fall of proud Mortimer:

As it was sundrie times publiquely acted
in the honourable citie of London, by the
right honourable the Earle of Pem—
brooke his seruants.

Written by Chri. Marlow *Gent.*

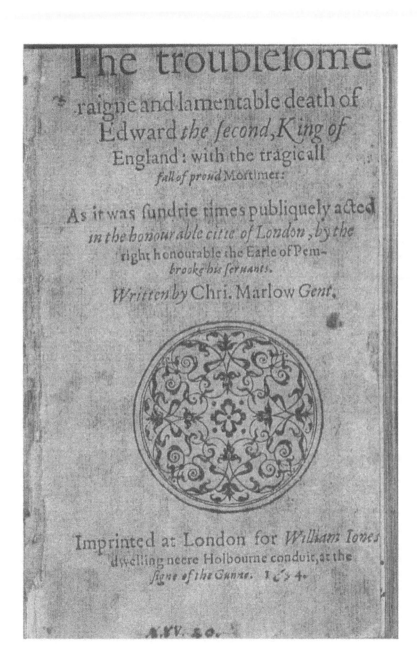

Imprinted at London for *William Iones*
dwelling neere Holbourne conduit, at the
signe of the Gunne. 1594.

DRAMATIS PERSONAE

EDWARD II, *King of England*
ISABELLA, *Queen of England, the King of France's sister*
PRINCE EDWARD, *their son, later King Edward III*
EDMUND, EARL OF KENT, *the King's brother*

The King's Favourites
PIERS GAVESTON, *later Earl of Cornwall*
SPENCER JUNIOR, *Lady Margaret's servant, later Earl of Gloucester*
SPENCER SENIOR, *his father, later Earl of Wiltshire and Marquess of Winchester*
BALDOCK, *a scholar, Lady Margaret's tutor*

The Barons
MORTIMER JUNIOR, *of Wigmore*
MORTIMER SENIOR, *of Chirke, his uncle*
THE EARL OF LANCASTER
GUY, EARL OF WARWICK
THE EARL OF PEMBROKE
LORD BEAUMONT
LADY MARGARET DE CLARE, *Gaveston's fiancée*
LORD MALTRAVERS, EARL OF ARUNDEL, *the King's ally, later his keeper*
THE EARL OF LEICESTER
LORD BERKELEY

The Church
THE BISHOP OF COVENTRY
THE BISHOP OF CANTERBURY
THE ABBOT OF NEATH
MONKS
THE BISHOP OF WINCHESTER

THREE POOR MEN
THE CLERK OF THE CROWN
PEMBROKE'S MEN
JAMES, *Pembroke's servant*
A HORSE-BOY, *Pembroke's servant*
LEVUNE, *a Frenchman*
A HERALD
SIR JOHN OF HAINAULT, *the Queen's ally*
RHYS AP HOWELL
THE MAYOR OF BRISTOL
A MOWER
TRUSSEL, *a representative of Parliament*
GOURNEY, *the King's keeper*
LIGHTBORNE, *an assassin*
THE KING'S CHAMPION
Lords, Attendants, Guards, Posts, Ladies-in-Waiting, Soldiers

EDWARD THE SECOND

[Scene 1]

Enter GAVESTON *reading on a letter that was brought
him from the King*

GAVESTON
'My father is deceased; come, Gaveston,
And share the kingdom with thy dearest friend.'
Ah, words that make me surfeit with delight!
What greater bliss can hap to Gaveston,
Than live and be the favourite of a king?   5
Sweet prince, I come; these, these thy amorous lines
Might have enforced me to have swum from France,
And, like Leander, gasped upon the sand,
So thou wouldst smile and take me in thy arms.
The sight of London to my exiled eyes   10
Is as Elysium to a new-come soul;
Not that I love the city or the men,
But that it harbours him I hold so dear,
The King, upon whose bosom let me die,
And with the world be still at enmity.   15
What need the arctic people love starlight,
To whom the sun shines both by day and night?
Farewell, base stooping to the lordly peers;
My knee shall bow to none but to the King.

The traditional act-divisions are not adopted in this edition: see the Note on the
    Text.
Head-title: ed. (The troublesome raigne and la- / *mentable death of* Edward *the* /
    second, king of England: with the / *tragicall fall of proud* Mortimer. Q)
  3 *surfeit* indulge, gorge
  4 *hap to* happen to; befall
  7 *France* Gaveston had been exiled by order of Edward I to his home in Gascony.
  8 *Leander* Tragic lover in the classical story retold in Marlowe's narrative poem
    Hero and Leander (c. 1593). Leander fell in love with Hero and swam the
    Hellespont to Sestos every night in order to be with her. One night the light in
    the tower which guided Leander to the Sestos shore was blown out by a storm
    and he drowned. Hero committed suicide when Leander's body was washed up
    on the shore.
11 *Elysium* the islands of the blessed in classical mythology; equivalent to heaven
14 *die* (i) swoon (ii) experience sexual orgasm

As for the multitude, that are but sparks   20
Raked up in embers of their poverty,
Tanti! I'll fan first on the wind
That glanceth at my lips and flieth away.

Enter three POOR MEN

But how now, what are these?
POOR MEN
Such as desire your worship's service.   25
GAVESTON
What canst thou do?
FIRST POOR MAN
I can ride.
GAVESTON
But I have no horses. What art thou?
SECOND POOR MAN
A traveller.
GAVESTON
Let me see, thou wouldst do well to wait at my trencher   30
and tell me lies at dinner-time; and, as I like your dis-
coursing, I'll have you. And what art thou?
THIRD POOR MAN
A soldier, that hath served against the Scot.
GAVESTON
Why, there are hospitals for such as you;

20–1 *multitude . . . poverty* Gaveston, for whom the King is like the sun, disdains
  the common people as mere dull embers – they have to be raked even to show
  sparks of life. Merchant sees this metaphor as 'an extended play on the relationship between the sun as the principal light of the heavens and kingship and degree among men'.
22 *Tanti!* 'So much for them!' (spoken with contempt)
22–3 *fan . . . flieth away* This image of blowing air to keep a fire's embers burning
  builds upon the imagery of lines 20–1; it also depicts Gaveston's impudent
  assumption that he can control the common people.
23 sd ed.; after line 24 in Q
27 sp FIRST POOR MAN ed. (*1. poore.* Q)
29 sp SECOND POOR MAN ed. (*2. poore.* Q)
30 ed. (*Let . . . well / To . . . time, / And . . . you. / And . . . thou?* Q)
  trencher wooden plate
31 *lies* travellers' tales. Cf. proverb, 'A traveller may lie with authority' (Tilley T
  476)
  as if
33 sp THIRD POOR MAN ed. (*3. poore.* Q)
  served . . . Scot England was troubled in the later years of Edward I's reign by a
  long war with Scotland, led by Robert Bruce.
34 *hospitals* charitable hospices for the needy

I have no war, and therefore, sir, be gone.   35
THIRD POOR MAN
  Farewell, and perish by a soldier's hand,
  That wouldst reward them with an hospital.
GAVESTON
  [*Aside*] Ay, ay. These words of his move me as much
  As if a goose should play the porcupine,
  And dart her plumes, thinking to pierce my breast.   40
  But yet it is no pain to speak men fair;
  I'll flatter these, and make them live in hope.
  [*To them*] You know that I came lately out of France,
  And yet I have not viewed my lord the King;
  If I speed well, I'll entertain you all.   45
POOR MEN
  We thank your worship.
GAVESTON
  I have some business; leave me to myself.
POOR MEN
  We will wait here about the court.   *Exeunt*
GAVESTON
  Do. These are not men for me;
  I must have wanton poets, pleasant wits,   50
  Musicians, that with touching of a string
  May draw the pliant King which way I please.
  Music and poetry is his delight;
  Therefore I'll have Italian masques by night,
  Sweet speeches, comedies, and pleasing shows;   55
  And in the day when he shall walk abroad,
  Like sylvan nymphs my pages shall be clad,

36 sp THIRD POOR MAN ed. (*Sold.* Q)
40 *dart . . . plumes* The Elizabethans believed that porcupines would shoot their
    quills in self-defence.
45 *speed well* am successful
    entertain take into service
46, 48 sp POOR MEN ed. (*Omnes.* Q)
50 *wanton* lascivious
    pleasant wits jocular, intelligent, and pleasing orators
52 *pliant* malleable, readily influenced
54 *masques* Courtly dramatic entertainments which originated in Italy and became
    popular in the English court during the late sixteenth and early seventeenth cen-
    turies. The earlier form of masque involved singing and dancing, in which the
    performers would be partially disguised by masks. The later development
    involved great costliness of scenes and costumes.
56 *abroad* outside, out of doors
57 *sylvan nymphs* female wood spirits

My men like satyrs grazing on the lawns
Shall with their goat-feet dance an antic hay;
Sometime a lovely boy in Dian's shape,   60
With hair that gilds the water as it glides,
Crownets of pearl about his naked arms,
And in his sportful hands an olive tree
To hide those parts which men delight to see,
Shall bathe him in a spring; and there hard by,   65
One like Actaeon peeping through the grove,
Shall by the angry goddess be transformed,
And running in the likeness of an hart,
By yelping hounds pulled down, and seem to die.
Such things as these best please his majesty.   70

Enter [EDWARD] *the King,* LANCASTER, MORTIMER SENIOR,
MORTIMER JUNIOR, EDMUND EARL OF KENT, GUY EARL OF
WARWICK[, *and attendants*]

My lord! Here comes the King and the nobles
From the parliament; I'll stand aside.
EDWARD
    Lancaster.
LANCASTER
    My lord.
GAVESTON
    [*Aside*] That Earl of Lancaster do I abhor.   75
EDWARD
    Will you not grant me this? [*Aside*] In spite of them
    I'll have my will, and these two Mortimers

58 *satyrs* woodland demons which are part-human, part-goat, and are usually
    associated with Bacchus, the classical god of wine and revelry
59 *antic* grotesque
    hay a country dance with a serpentine movement
60 *Dian's shape* i.e. the appearance of Diana; in classical mythology, the moon
    goddess who was also associated with female chastity
61 *gilds . . . glides* i.e. covers the water with a golden colour. This image could also
    imply artifice: cf. Holland's trans. Pliny's *Naturalis Historia* (1601), 'I see that
    now adaies siluer only . . . is guilded by the means of this artificiall Quicksiluer.'
62 *Crownets* coronets
63 *sportful* playful, sportive
65 *hard by* close by, near
66 *Actaeon* In classical mythology, the hunter who offended the goddess Diana by
    seeing her bathe naked. In her anger, she turned him into a stag, and he was later
    chased and killed by his own hounds. Cf. Ovid's *Metamorphoses*, III. 138ff.
70 sd ed.: after line 72 in Q
72 *stand aside* Gaveston withdraws to the side of the stage until line 138.

That cross me thus shall know I am displeased.

MORTIMER SENIOR

If you love us, my lord, hate Gaveston.

GAVESTON

[*Aside*] That villain Mortimer, I'll be his death.   80

MORTIMER JUNIOR

Mine uncle here, this earl, and I myself
Were sworn to your father at his death,
That he should ne'er return into the realm;
And know, my lord, ere I will break my oath,
This sword of mine that should offend your foes,   85
Shall sleep within the scabbard at thy need,
And underneath thy banners march who will,
For Mortimer will hang his armour up.

GAVESTON

[*Aside*] *Mort Dieu*!

EDWARD

Well Mortimer, I'll make thee rue these words.   90
Beseems it thee to contradict thy King?
Frownst thou thereat, aspiring Lancaster?
The sword shall plane the furrows of thy brows
And hew these knees that now are grown so stiff.
I will have Gaveston; and you shall know   95
What danger 'tis to stand against your King.

GAVESTON

[*Aside*] Well done, Ned.

LANCASTER

My lord, why do you thus incense your peers
That naturally would love and honour you,
But for that base and obscure Gaveston?   100
Four earldoms have I besides Lancaster:
Derby, Salisbury, Lincoln, Leicester.
These will I sell to give my soldiers pay,
Ere Gaveston shall stay within the realm.

78 *cross* obstruct
87 *banners* fringed flags which were carried as standards before an army
89 *Mort Dieu*! A French oath meaning 'by God's death', reminding us of
    Gaveston's Continental origins.
90 *rue* regret
91 *Beseems it thee* i.e. is it fitting for you
92 *thereat* at that
97 *Ned* This diminutive emphasizes Gaveston's familiar relationship with the King.
99 *naturally* by nature, by birth (according to their social status)
100 *base* of low birth, poor stock
    obscure lowly

Therefore if he be come, expel him straight.   105
KENT
Barons and earls, your pride hath made me mute.
But now I'll speak, and to the proof I hope:
I do remember in my father's days,
Lord Percy of the North, being highly moved,
Braved Mowbery in presence of the King.   110
For which, had not his highness loved him well,
He should have lost his head, but with his look
The undaunted spirit of Percy was appeased,
And Mowbery and he were reconciled.
Yet dare you brave the King unto his face?   115
Brother, revenge it; and let these their heads
Preach upon poles for trespass of their tongues.
WARWICK
O, our heads!
EDWARD
Ay, yours; and therefore I would wish you grant.
WARWICK
Bridle thy anger, gentle Mortimer.   120
MORTIMER JUNIOR
I cannot, nor I will not; I must speak.
Cousin, our hands I hope shall fence our heads,
And strike off his that makes you threaten us.
Come uncle, let us leave the brainsick King,
And henceforth parley with our naked swords.   125
MORTIMER SENIOR
Welshry hath men enough to save our heads.

106 sp KENT ed. (*Edm.* Q; and throughout the text whenever '*Edm.*' is used)
107 *to the proof* irrefutably
109 *moved* angry
110 *Braved* challenged
     Mowbery Mowbray (*Mowberie* Q; also at line 114)
117 *Preach . . . poles* After execution, traitors' severed heads were publicly displayed
     on poles as a warning to others.
119 *grant* assent
122 *Cousin* A term used by a sovereign when formally addressing a nobleman. In this
     instance Mortimer Junior, being Edward's subject, uses the term presumptu-
     ously.
     fence shield
126 *Welshry* ed. (Wilshire Q) the Welsh populace. Roma Gill has pointed out that the
     policy of most editors to adopt the reading 'Wiltshire' is historically incorrect and
     may well have been a compositorial misreading for 'Welshrye'. Mortimer Senior
     was in fact Edward's Lieutenant and Justice of Wales, governing Wales from
     1307 to 1321. See 'Mortimer's Men', *N&Q*, n.s. 27 (1980), 159.

WARWICK
All Warwickshire will love him for my sake.
LANCASTER
And northward Gaveston hath many friends.
Adieu my lord; and either change your mind,
Or look to see the throne where you should sit   130
To float in blood, and at thy wanton head
The glozing head of thy base minion thrown.

Exeunt NOBLES [*except* KENT]

EDWARD
I cannot brook these haughty menaces:
Am I a king and must be overruled?
Brother, display my ensigns in the field;   135
I'll bandy with the barons and the earls,
And either die or live with Gaveston.
GAVESTON
I can no longer keep me from my lord.   [*He steps forward*]
EDWARD
What, Gaveston! Welcome! Kiss not my hand;
Embrace me, Gaveston, as I do thee!   140
Why shouldst thou kneel; knowest thou not who I am?
Thy friend, thy self, another Gaveston!
Not Hylas was more mourned of Hercules
Than thou hast been of me since thy exile.
GAVESTON
And since I went from hence, no soul in hell   145
Hath felt more torment than poor Gaveston.
EDWARD
I know it. [*To* KENT] Brother, welcome home my friend.

128 spoken ironically, like the previous line: Lancaster means Gaveston has no
     friends at all in the north
132 *glozing* flattering
     minion A powerful man's favourite or homosexual lover; derived from the
     French *mignon* (= sweet), applied to the favourites of Henry III of France.
133 *brook* endure
     menaces threats
135 *ensigns* military banners
     in the field in battle
136 *bandy* give and take blows, as in a game of tennis
141 ed. (Why . . . kneele, / Knowest . . . I am? Q)
143 *Hylas . . . Hercules* Hylas accompanied Hercules on the journey of the
     Argonauts. When they anchored at Mysia, Hylas was carried away by water-
     nymphs. In his grief, Hercules remained behind, searching for the lost boy whilst
     the Argonauts continued their journey.

[*To* GAVESTON] Now let the treacherous Mortimers
    conspire,
And that high-minded Earl of Lancaster.
I have my wish, in that I joy thy sight,   150
And sooner shall the sea o'erwhelm my land
Than bear the ship that shall transport thee hence.
I here create thee Lord High Chamberlain,
Chief Secretary to the state and me,
Earl of Cornwall, King and Lord of Man.   155

GAVESTON
My lord, these titles far exceed my worth.

KENT
Brother, the least of these may well suffice
For one of greater birth than Gaveston.

EDWARD
Cease, brother, for I cannot brook these words.
[*To* GAVESTON] Thy worth, sweet friend, is far above my   160
    gifts,
Therefore to equal it, receive my heart.
If for these dignities thou be envied,
I'll give thee more, for but to honour thee
Is Edward pleased with kingly regiment.
Fear'st thou thy person? Thou shalt have a guard.   165
Wants thou gold? Go to my treasury.
Wouldst thou be loved and feared? Receive my seal,
Save or condemn, and in our name command
What so thy mind affects or fancy likes.

GAVESTON
It shall suffice me to enjoy your love,   170
Which whiles I have, I think myself as great
As Caesar riding in the Roman street,
With captive kings at his triumphant car.

Enter the BISHOP OF COVENTRY

---

149 *high-minded* arrogant   150 *joy* enjoy
155 *King . . . Man* Until 1829, the rulers of The Isle of Man were known as kings,
    possessing certain sovereign rights (Gill).
164 *regiment* rule
167 *seal* A token of royal authority; in performance the seal is often in the form of a
    ring.
169 *affects* desires
    fancy (i) caprice (ii) amorous inclination
172–3 *Caesar . . . kings* A popular image of conquest. Cf. George Peele's *Edward I*,
    'Not Caesar leading through the streetes of Rome, / The captive kings of con-
    quered nations, / Was in his princely triumphes honoured more' (i. 91–3).
173 *car* chariot

EDWARD
Whither goes my lord of Coventry so fast?
BISHOP OF COVENTRY
To celebrate your father's exequies.   175
But is that wicked Gaveston returned?
EDWARD
Ay, priest, and lives to be revenged on thee
That wert the only cause of his exile.
GAVESTON
'Tis true, and but for reverence of these robes
Thou shouldst not plod one foot beyond this place.   180
BISHOP OF COVENTRY
I did no more than I was bound to do;
And Gaveston, unless thou be reclaimed,
As then I did incense the parliament,
So will I now, and thou shalt back to France.
GAVESTON
Saving your reverence, you must pardon me.   185
EDWARD
Throw off his golden mitre, rend his stole,
And in the channel christen him anew.

                              [*Assaults* COVENTRY]

KENT
Ah brother, lay not violent hands on him,
For he'll complain unto the See of Rome.
GAVESTON
Let him complain unto the See of Hell;   190
I'll be revenged on him for my exile.
EDWARD
No, spare his life, but seize upon his goods.

---

175 sp BISHOP OF COVENTRY ed. (*Bish.* Q; also at ll. 181, 198, and 200)
     exequies funeral rites
182 *reclaimed* reformed, subdued
183 *incense* incite
185 *Saving your reverence* a sarcastic rendering of a proverbial expression which was
     usually said apologetically (Tilley R 93)
186 *golden mitre* head-dress which was a symbol of episcopal office; rarely worn in the
     Anglican Church after the Reformation
     rend tear
     stole ecclesiastical vestment
187 *channel* gutter. For the exact nature of the violence done to the Bishop, cf. 2.
     35–6.
189 *See of Rome* i.e. the Pope
192 *goods* property, possessions

Be thou lord bishop, and receive his rents,
And make him serve thee as thy chaplain.
I give him thee; here, use him as thou wilt.   195
GAVESTON
He shall to prison, and there die in bolts.
EDWARD
Ay, to the Tower, the Fleet, or where thou wilt.
BISHOP OF COVENTRY
For this offence be thou accurst of God.
EDWARD
Who's there?

[Enter guards]

Convey this priest to the Tower.
BISHOP OF COVENTRY
True, true!   *[Exit* BISHOP *and guards]*   200
EDWARD
But in the meantime Gaveston, away,
And take possession of his house and goods.
Come, follow me, and thou shalt have my guard
To see it done and bring thee safe again.
GAVESTON
What should a priest do with so fair a house?   205
A prison may beseem his holiness.   *[Exeunt]*

[Scene 2]

Enter both the MORTIMERS *[on one side]*, WARWICK, *and*
LANCASTER *[on the other]*

WARWICK
'Tis true, the Bishop is in the Tower,
And goods and body given to Gaveston.

193 *rents* (i) revenues, income (ii) taxes levied by the Church
196 *bolts* fetters
197 *the Fleet* in Marlowe's time, a prison which stood between the River Thames and
       Ludgate Hill
198 *accurst* doomed to damnation
199 *Convey* conduct, escort
203 *guard* (i) body of soldiers (ii) guardianship, safe conduct
205 *fair* fine, beautiful
206 *beseem* be fitting, more appropriate (because of the meagre conditions which are
       commonly associated with a priest's cell)

  0 sd Characters usually entered the Elizabethan stage through two or more doors
       set into the rear wall. Entry through different doors (as editorially indicated
       here) signified that they had come from different directions.

LANCASTER
What, will they tyrannize upon the Church?
Ah, wicked King! Accursèd Gaveston!
This ground which is corrupted with their steps   5
Shall be their timeless sepulchre, or mine.
MORTIMER JUNIOR
Well, let that peevish Frenchman guard him sure;
Unless his breast be sword-proof he shall die.
MORTIMER SENIOR
How now, why droops the Earl of Lancaster?
MORTIMER JUNIOR
Wherefore is Guy of Warwick discontent?   10
LANCASTER
That villain Gaveston is made an earl.
MORTIMER SENIOR
An earl!
WARWICK
Ay, and besides, Lord Chamberlain of the realm,
And Secretary too, and Lord of Man.
MORTIMER SENIOR
We may not, nor we will not suffer this.   15
MORTIMER JUNIOR
Why post we not from hence to levy men?
LANCASTER
'My Lord of Cornwall' now at every word;
And happy is the man whom he vouchsafes
For vailing of his bonnet one good look.
Thus, arm in arm, the King and he doth march –   20
Nay more, the guard upon his lordship waits,
And all the court begins to flatter him.
WARWICK
Thus leaning on the shoulder of the King,
He nods, and scorns, and smiles at those that pass.

3 *tyrannize* Edward is acting tyrannically in that, by imprisoning the Bishop, he is
usurping the spiritual power of the Church.
6 *timeless* (i) eternal (ii) untimely
   sepulchre tomb, grave
7 *peevish* foolish   *him* himself   *sure* securely
11 *villain* (i) rascal, scoundrel (ii) serf, bondman (deriving from 'villein', one of low
birth)
15 *suffer* tolerate
16 *post* i.e. travel with speed
    levy men assemble soldiers
19 *vailing* doffing
24 *scorns* mocks

MORTIMER SENIOR
   Doth no man take exceptions at the slave?   25
LANCASTER
   All stomach him, but none dare speak a word.
MORTIMER JUNIOR
   Ah, that bewrays their baseness, Lancaster.
   Were all the earls and barons of my mind,
   We'll hale him from the bosom of the King,
   And at the court gate hang the peasant up,   30
   Who, swoll'n with venom of ambitious pride,
   Will be the ruin of the realm and us.

Enter the BISHOP OF CANTERBURY[, *talking to an* ATTENDANT]

WARWICK
   Here comes my lord of Canterbury's grace.
LANCASTER
   His countenance bewrays he is displeased.
BISHOP OF CANTERBURY [*To* ATTENDANT]
   First were his sacred garments rent and torn,   35
   Then laid they violent hands upon him next,
   Himself imprisoned and his goods asseized;
   This certify the Pope. Away, take horse.

                               [*Exit* ATTENDANT]

LANCASTER
   My lord, will you take arms against the King?
BISHOP OF CANTERBURY
   What need I? God himself is up in arms   40
   When violence is offered to the Church.
MORTIMER JUNIOR
   Then will you join with us that be his peers
   To banish or behead that Gaveston?

26 *stomach* resent
27 *bewrays* reveals
29 *hale* draw, drag
31 *Who . . . pride* Cf. *Dr Faustus*, 'Till, swoll'n with cunning of a self-conceit'
   (A-Text, Prologue, 20).
33 *grace* i.e. his grace (formal term of address)
34 *countenance* face, demeanour
   bewrays betrays
35 sp BISHOP OF CANTERBURY ed. (*Bish.* Q; also at ll. 40, 44, 61, 68 and 75)
37 *asseized* seized
38 *certify* inform (with certainty)

BISHOP OF CANTERBURY
　What else, my lords? For it concerns me near;
　The bishopric of Coventry is his.　　　　　　　　45

Enter [ISABELLA] *the Queen*

MORTIMER JUNIOR
　Madam, whither walks your majesty so fast?
ISABELLA
　Unto the forest, gentle Mortimer,
　To live in grief and baleful discontent;
　For now my lord the King regards me not,
　But dotes upon the love of Gaveston.　　　　　50
　He claps his cheeks and hangs about his neck,
　Smiles in his face and whispers in his ears;
　And when I come he frowns, as who should say,
　'Go whither thou wilt, seeing I have Gaveston.'
MORTIMER SENIOR
　Is it not strange that he is thus bewitched?　　55
MORTIMER JUNIOR
　Madam, return unto the court again.
　That sly inveigling Frenchman we'll exile,
　Or lose our lives; and yet, ere that day come,
　The King shall lose his crown, for we have power
　And courage too, to be revenged at full.　　　60
BISHOP OF CANTERBURY
　But yet lift not your swords against the King.
LANCASTER
　No, but we'll lift Gaveston from hence.
WARWICK
　And war must be the means, or he'll stay still.
ISABELLA
　Then let him stay; for rather than my lord
　Shall be oppressed by civil mutinies,　　　　　65

44　*near* (i) deeply (ii) personally (in that, by becoming a bishop, Gaveston becomes
　　a matter of direct concern to Canterbury)
45　*bishopric* diocese
47　sp ISABELLA ed. (*Que.*Q; and throughout the play text)
　　forest wastelands; a metaphorical expression which describes Isabella's feelings of
　　isolation　*gentle* kind
48　*baleful* wretched　　49　*regards* considers
51　*claps* slaps affectionately
57　*inveigling* deceiving　　58　*ere* before
62　*lift* (i) steal (ii) raise (by hanging)
63　*still* always

I will endure a melancholy life,
And let him frolic with his minion.

BISHOP OF CANTERBURY
My lords, to ease all this but hear me speak.
We and the rest that are his councillors
Will meet and with a general consent   70
Confirm his banishment with our hands and seals.

LANCASTER
What we confirm the King will frustrate.

MORTIMER JUNIOR
Then may we lawfully revolt from him.

WARWICK
But say, my lord, where shall this meeting be?

BISHOP OF CANTERBURY
At the New Temple.   75

MORTIMER JUNIOR
Content.

BISHOP OF CANTERBURY
And in the meantime I'll entreat you all
To cross to Lambeth, and there stay with me.

LANCASTER
Come then, let's away.

MORTIMER JUNIOR
Madam, farewell.   80

ISABELLA
Farewell, sweet Mortimer; and for my sake,
Forbear to levy arms against the King.

MORTIMER JUNIOR
Ay, if words will serve; if not, I must.   [*Exeunt*]

[Scene 3]

Enter GAVESTON *and the* EARL OF KENT

GAVESTON
Edmund, the mighty prince of Lancaster,
That hath more earldoms than an ass can bear,

---

67 *frolic* make merry (with overtones of sexual promiscuity)
68 *but* only   72 *frustrate* annul, defeat
75 *New Temple* A building established and used by the Knights Templar until their
    suppression in 1308.
77 sp BISHOP OF CANTERBURY ed. (not in Q); (*Mor. iu.* Content. And . . . all, / To
    crosse . . . me. Q)
78 *Lambeth* Lambeth Palace, the official residence of the Archbishop of Canterbury

1 Gaveston addresses Kent familiarly by his personal name

And both the Mortimers, two goodly men,
With Guy of Warwick, that redoubted knight,
Are gone towards Lambeth; there let them remain.   5

Exeunt

[Scene 4]

Enter NOBLES [LANCASTER, WARWICK, PEMBROKE, MORTIMER
SENIOR, MORTIMER JUNIOR, *and the* BISHOP OF CANTERBURY,
with attendants]

LANCASTER
Here is the form of Gaveston's exile;
May it please your lordship to subscribe your name.
BISHOP OF CANTERBURY
Give me the paper.
LANCASTER
Quick, quick, my lord; I long to write my name.
WARWICK
But I long more to see him banished hence.   5
MORTIMER JUNIOR
The name of Mortimer shall fright the King,
Unless he be declined from that base peasant.

Enter [EDWARD] *the King and* GAVESTON[, *with* KENT]
[EDWARD *assumes the throne, with* GAVESTON *at his side*]

EDWARD
What, are you moved that Gaveston sits here?
It is our pleasure; we will have it so.
LANCASTER
Your grace doth well to place him by your side,   10
For nowhere else the new Earl is so safe.

---

4 *redoubted* feared

0 sd Q uses the terms 'nobles' and 'barons' indifferently to refer to the rebel lords.
1 *form* document
3 sp BISHOP OF CANTERBURY ed. (*Bish.* Q; and throughout the scene)
7 *declined* turned aside
8 *sits here* 'Gaveston's seat beside the king (where the queen would normally sit) is
   both emblematic and shocking; it signifies that Edward has made his lover
   politically equal with himself' (Forker).
9 *pleasure* will
11 *new Earl* The emphasis on 'new' reiterates the nobles' annoyance that such an
   'upstart' has acquired, not inherited, his aristocratic status.

MORTIMER SENIOR
  What man of noble birth can brook this sight?
  Quam male conveniunt!
  See what a scornful look the peasant casts.
PEMBROKE
  Can kingly lions fawn on creeping ants?   15
WARWICK
  Ignoble vassal, that like Phaëthon
  Aspir'st unto the guidance of the sun.
MORTIMER JUNIOR
  Their downfall is at hand, their forces down;
  We will not thus be faced and over-peered.
EDWARD
  Lay hands on that traitor Mortimer!   20
MORTIMER SENIOR
  Lay hands on that traitor Gaveston!

                          [*The* NOBLES *draw swords*]

KENT
  Is this the duty that you owe your King?
WARWICK
  We know our duties; let him know his peers.

                          [*The* NOBLES *seize* GAVESTON]

EDWARD
  Whither will you bear him? Stay, or ye shall die.
MORTIMER SENIOR
  We are no traitors, therefore threaten not.   25
GAVESTON
  No, threaten not, my lord, but pay them home.
  Were I a king –

---

13 *Quam male conveniunt!* How badly they go together (i.e. match, suit one
   another)! Derived from Ovid's *Metamorphoses*, II. 846–7.
14 *scornful* derisive, contemptuous
16 *Ignoble* of low birth
   vassal slave
   Phaëthon In classical mythology, the son of Phoebus Apollo (the sun god), who
   ignored warnings not to drive his father's chariot, lost control, and caused dev-
   astation on earth before the chariot was destroyed by Jupiter. In the sixteenth
   century, the story was commonly used as an emblem of the fall of overweening
   ambition. Cf. Ovid's *Metamorphoses*, I. 755ff.
19 *faced* bullied
   over-peered looked down upon (with pun on 'peer' = nobleman)
24 *bear* conduct, take
26 *pay them home* chastise them

MORTIMER JUNIOR
Thou villain, wherefore talks thou of a king,
That hardly art a gentleman by birth?
EDWARD
Were he a peasant, being my minion,   30
I'll make the proudest of you stoop to him.
LANCASTER
My lord, you may not thus disparage us.
Away, I say, with hateful Gaveston.
MORTIMER SENIOR
And with the Earl of Kent that favours him.

                        [*Exeunt* GAVESTON *and* KENT *guarded*]

EDWARD
Nay, then lay violent hands upon your King.   35
Here, Mortimer, sit thou in Edward's throne;
Warwick and Lancaster, wear you my crown.
Was ever king thus overruled as I?
LANCASTER
Learn then to rule us better and the realm.
MORTIMER JUNIOR
What we have done, our heart-blood shall maintain.   40
WARWICK
Think you that we can brook this upstart pride?
EDWARD
Anger and wrathful fury stops my speech.
BISHOP OF CANTERBURY
Why are you moved? Be patient, my lord,
And see what we your councillors have done.

        [*He presents the document of* GAVESTON'S *exile to* EDWARD]

MORTIMER JUNIOR
My lords, now let us all be resolute,   45
And either have our wills or lose our lives.
EDWARD
Meet you for this, proud overdaring peers?
Ere my sweet Gaveston shall part from me,
This isle shall fleet upon the ocean
And wander to the unfrequented Inde.   50

---

32 *disparage* vilify; 'originally meant to degrade by marrying to one of inferior rank'
     (Charlton and Waller)
47 *overdaring* imprudent, foolhardy
49 *fleet* float
50 *Inde* East Indies

BISHOP OF CANTERBURY
You know that I am legate to the Pope;
On your allegiance to the See of Rome,
Subscribe as we have done to his exile.
MORTIMER JUNIOR
Curse him if he refuse, and then may we
Depose him and elect another king.   55
EDWARD
Ay, there it goes, but yet I will not yield.
Curse me. Depose me. Do the worst you can.
LANCASTER
Then linger not, my lord, but do it straight.
BISHOP OF CANTERBURY
Remember how the Bishop was abused;
Either banish him that was the cause thereof,   60
Or I will presently discharge these lords
Of duty and allegiance due to thee.
EDWARD
It boots me not to threat; I must speak fair,
The legate of the Pope will be obeyed.
My lord, you shall be Chancellor of the realm;   65
Thou Lancaster, High Admiral of our fleet.
Young Mortimer and his uncle shall be earls,
And you, Lord Warwick, President of the North,
[To PEMBROKE] And thou of Wales. If this content you not,
Make several kingdoms of this monarchy,   70
And share it equally amongst you all,
So I may have some nook or corner left
To frolic with my dearest Gaveston.
BISHOP OF CANTERBURY
Nothing shall alter us; we are resolved.
LANCASTER
Come, come, subscribe.   75
MORTIMER JUNIOR
Why should you love him whom the world hates so?

---

51 *legate* deputy, representative
54 *Curse* excommunicate
59 *abused* insulted, ill-used (violently)
61–2 The subjects of an excommunicated monarch were absolved of their duty of obedience; Elizabeth I had been excommunicated by Pope Pius V in 1570.
63 *boots* avails
68 *President of the North* Gill cites John Cowell's *The Interpreter* (1607): '*President . . .* is used in Common law for the kings Lieutenant in any Province or function; as President of Wales, of York, of Barwick.'

EDWARD
Because he loves me more than all the world.
Ah, none but rude and savage-minded men
Would seek the ruin of my Gaveston;
You that be noble born should pity him.   80
WARWICK
You that are princely born should shake him off.
For shame subscribe, and let the lown depart.
MORTIMER SENIOR
Urge him, my lord.
BISHOP OF CANTERBURY
Are you content to banish him the realm?
EDWARD
I see I must, and therefore am content;   85
Instead of ink, I'll write it with my tears.

                              [*He signs the document*]

MORTIMER JUNIOR
The King is love-sick for his minion.
EDWARD
'Tis done, and now accursèd hand fall off.
LANCASTER
Give it me; I'll have it published in the streets.
MORTIMER JUNIOR
I'll see him presently dispatched away.   90
BISHOP OF CANTERBURY
Now is my heart at ease.
WARWICK   And so is mine.
PEMBROKE
This will be good news to the common sort.
MORTIMER SENIOR
Be it or no, he shall not linger here.

     Exeunt NOBLES[, *the* BISHOP OF CANTERBURY, *and attendants*]

EDWARD
How fast they run to banish him I love;
They would not stir, were it to do me good.   95
Why should a king be subject to a priest?
Proud Rome, that hatchest such imperial grooms,

78 *rude* uncivilized
82 *lown* peasant
89 *published* proclaimed
90 *presently* immediately
92 *common sort* i.e. the common people
95 *stir* act
97 *imperial* imperious   *grooms* servants

For these thy superstitious taper-lights,
Wherewith thy antichristian churches blaze,
I'll fire thy crazèd buildings and enforce   100
The papal towers to kiss the lowly ground,
With slaughtered priests make Tiber's channel swell,
And banks raised higher with their sepulchres.
As for the peers that back the clergy thus,
If I be King, not one of them shall live.   105

Enter GAVESTON

GAVESTON
My lord, I hear it whispered everywhere
That I am banished and must fly the land.
EDWARD
'Tis true, sweet Gaveston. O were it false!
The legate of the Pope will have it so,
And thou must hence, or I shall be deposed.   110
But I will reign to be revenged of them,
And therefore, sweet friend, take it patiently.
Live where thou wilt – I'll send thee gold enough.
And long thou shalt not stay, or if thou dost,
I'll come to thee; my love shall ne'er decline.   115
GAVESTON
Is all my hope turned to this hell of grief?
EDWARD
Rend not my heart with thy too-piercing words.
Thou from this land, I from my self am banished.
GAVESTON
To go from hence grieves not poor Gaveston,
But to forsake you, in whose gracious looks   120
The blessedness of Gaveston remains,
For nowhere else seeks he felicity.
EDWARD
And only this torments my wretched soul,
That whether I will or no, thou must depart.
Be Governor of Ireland in my stead,   125
And there abide till fortune call thee home.
Here, take my picture, and let me wear thine.

[*They exchange miniatures*]

---

98 *taper-lights* candles for devotional and penitential use
100 *crazèd* shattered, unsound. Cf. *Massacre at Paris*, 'I'll fire his crazèd buildings,
    and incense / The papal towers to kiss the holy earth' (xxiv. 62–3)
102 *make* ed. (may Q)
    Tiber's channel the River Tiber in Rome
121 *blessedness* superlative happiness

O might I keep thee here, as I do this,
Happy were I, but now most miserable.
GAVESTON
'Tis something to be pitied of a king.   130
EDWARD
Thou shalt not hence; I'll hide thee, Gaveston.
GAVESTON
I shall be found, and then 'twill grieve me more.
EDWARD
Kind words and mutual talk makes our grief greater.
Therefore, with dumb embracement, let us part –
Stay, Gaveston, I cannot leave thee thus.   135
GAVESTON
For every look my lord drops down a tear;
Seeing I must go, do not renew my sorrow.
EDWARD
The time is little that thou hast to stay,
And therefore give me leave to look my fill.
But come, sweet friend, I'll bear thee on thy way.   140
GAVESTON
The peers will frown.
EDWARD
I pass not for their anger; come, let's go.
O that we might as well return as go.

          Enter EDMUND [EARL OF KENT] *and Queen* ISABELLA

ISABELLA
Whither goes my lord?
EDWARD
Fawn not on me, French strumpet; get thee gone.   145

131 *hence* i.e. go
134 *dumb* silent
140 *bear* accompany
142 *pass* care
143 sd ed. (*Enter Edmund and Queen Isabell.* Q) Kent has no lines, and there is a
     problem in finding a suitable point for him to exit. Other editors have reasoned
     that his presence is superfluous, detracting from the dramatic tension between
     the three lovers, and have deleted him from the stage direction. However, his
     presence as a silent witness to Edward's behaviour contributes a political di-
     mension to an otherwise exclusively personal sequence, and helps to clarify the
     character's confused loyalties and subsequent changing allegiances.
145 *strumpet* sexually loose woman, prostitute

ISABELLA
On whom but on my husband should I fawn?
GAVESTON
On Mortimer, with whom, ungentle Queen –
I say no more; judge you the rest, my lord.
ISABELLA
In saying this, thou wrongst me, Gaveston.
Is't not enough that thou corrupts my lord,   150
And art a bawd to his affections,
But thou must call mine honour thus in question?
GAVESTON
I mean not so; your grace must pardon me.
EDWARD
Thou art too familiar with that Mortimer,
And by thy means is Gaveston exiled;   155
But I would wish thee reconcile the lords,
Or thou shalt ne'er be reconciled to me.
ISABELLA
Your highness knows it lies not in my power.
EDWARD
Away then, touch me not; come Gaveston.
ISABELLA
Villain, 'tis thou that robb'st me of my lord.   160
GAVESTON
Madam, 'tis you that rob me of my lord.
EDWARD
Speak not unto her; let her droop and pine.
ISABELLA
Wherein, my lord, have I deserved these words?
Witness the tears that Isabella sheds,
Witness this heart, that sighing for thee breaks,   165
How dear my lord is to poor Isabel.
EDWARD
And witness heaven how dear thou art to me.

147 Gaveston makes the first insinuation of adultery between Isabella and Mortimer
    Junior.
149 To accuse a woman unjustly of sexual misconduct was a grave misdemeanour in
    Elizabethan England.
150 *my lord* implying 'husband' as well as 'sovereign'
151 *bawd* procurer, pander
    affections (i) desires, inclinations (ii) passions (with sexual overtones)
163 *Wherein* in what
167 *witness . . . to me* At this point many productions have Edward and Gaveston
    embrace or kiss as lovers.

There weep; for till my Gaveston be repealed,
Assure thyself thou com'st not in my sight.

Exeunt EDWARD *and* GAVESTON[; *exit* KENT *at the other door*]

ISABELLA
O miserable and distressèd Queen!   170
Would when I left sweet France and was embarked,
That charming Circe, walking on the waves,
Had changed my shape, or at the marriage-day
The cup of Hymen had been full of poison,
Or with those arms that twined about my neck   175
I had been stifled, and not lived to see
The King my lord thus to abandon me.
Like frantic Juno will I fill the earth
With ghostly murmur of my sighs and cries,
For never doted Jove on Ganymede   180
So much as he on cursèd Gaveston.
But that will more exasperate his wrath;
I must entreat him, I must speak him fair,
And be a means to call home Gaveston.
And yet he'll ever dote on Gaveston,   185
And so am I forever miserable.

Enter the NOBLES [LANCASTER, WARWICK, PEMBROKE,
MORTIMER SENIOR, *and* MORTIMER JUNIOR] *to*
[ISABELLA] *the Queen*

LANCASTER
Look where the sister of the King of France
Sits wringing of her hands and beats her breast.
WARWICK
The King, I fear, hath ill entreated her.

168 *repealed* recalled from exile
169 sd *the other door* cf. 2. 0 sd n.
172 *Circe* witch who turned Odysseus' men into pigs. See Homer's *Odyssey*, X and
    Ovid's *Metamorphoses*, XIV. 48ff.
174 *Hymen* god of marriage
175 *those arms* i.e. Edward's arms (embracing Isabella)
178–80 *frantic Juno . . . Ganymede* In classical mythology, Juno became jealous when
    her husband Jove chose Ganymede to be his cup-bearer on account of his
    beauty. Marlowe dramatizes this homoerotic liaison in *Dido, Queen of Carthage*,
    I.i. See also Ovid's *Metamorphoses*, X. 155–61.
179 *murmur* (i) rumour (ii) expression of discontent
182 *exasperate* irritate, aggravate
183 *entreat* negotiate with   *fair* with kindness, courteously
185 *ever* always   189 *entreated* treated

PEMBROKE
  Hard is the heart that injures such a saint.   190
MORTIMER JUNIOR
  I know 'tis long of Gaveston she weeps.
MORTIMER SENIOR
  Why? He is gone.
MORTIMER JUNIOR   Madam, how fares your grace?
ISABELLA
  Ah, Mortimer! Now breaks the King's hate forth,
  And he confesseth that he loves me not.
MORTIMER JUNIOR
  Cry quittance, madam, then; and love not him.   195
ISABELLA
  No, rather will I die a thousand deaths.
  And yet I love in vain; he'll ne'er love me.
LANCASTER
  Fear ye not, madam; now his minion's gone,
  His wanton humour will be quickly left.
ISABELLA
  O never, Lancaster! I am enjoined   200
  To sue unto you all for his repeal.
  This wills my lord, and this must I perform
  Or else be banished from his highness' presence.
LANCASTER
  For his repeal! Madam, he comes not back
  Unless the sea cast up his shipwrack body.   205
WARWICK
  And to behold so sweet a sight as that
  There's none here but would run his horse to death.
MORTIMER JUNIOR
  But madam, would you have us call him home?
ISABELLA
  Ay, Mortimer, for till he be restored,
  The angry King hath banished me the court;   210
  And therefore, as thou lovest and tend'rest me,
  Be thou my advocate unto these peers.

---

191 *long of* on account of
195 *Cry quittance* (i) retaliate (ii) renounce the marriage bond (legal terminology)
199 *humour* temperament, disposition. The Elizabethans believed that humours or
    bodily fluids (phlegm, blood, choler, melancholy) were responsible for the state
    of a person's mind and body.
200 *enjoined* obliged, bound by oath
201 *sue* beg
205 *cast* throw up, vomit   *shipwrack* shipwrecked
211 *tend'rest* care for

MORTIMER JUNIOR
What, would ye have me plead for Gaveston?
MORTIMER SENIOR
Plead for him he that will, I am resolved.
LANCASTER
And so am I; my lord, dissuade the Queen.   215
ISABELLA
O Lancaster, let him dissuade the King,
For 'tis against my will he should return.
WARWICK
Then speak not for him; let the peasant go.
ISABELLA
'Tis for myself I speak, and not for him.
PEMBROKE
No speaking will prevail, and therefore cease.   220
MORTIMER JUNIOR
Fair Queen, forbear to angle for the fish
Which, being caught, strikes him that takes it dead –
I mean that vile torpedo, Gaveston,
That now, I hope, floats on the Irish seas.
ISABELLA
Sweet Mortimer, sit down by me a while,   225
And I will tell thee reasons of such weight
As thou wilt soon subscribe to his repeal.
MORTIMER JUNIOR
It is impossible; but speak your mind.
ISABELLA
Then thus – but none shall hear it but ourselves.

[ISABELLA *and* MORTIMER JUNIOR *talk apart*]

LANCASTER
My lords, albeit the Queen win Mortimer,   230
Will you be resolute and hold with me?
MORTIMER SENIOR
Not I, against my nephew.
PEMBROKE
Fear not, the Queen's words cannot alter him.
WARWICK
No? Do but mark how earnestly she pleads.

223 *torpedo* electric ray, cramp-fish
224 *floats* sails
226 *weight* importance
234 *mark* observe

LANCASTER
And see how coldly his looks make denial.   235
WARWICK
She smiles! Now, for my life, his mind is changed.
LANCASTER
I'll rather lose his friendship, I, than grant.
MORTIMER JUNIOR
[*Returning to them*] Well, of necessity, it must be so.
My lords, that I abhor base Gaveston
I hope your honours make no question;   240
And therefore, though I plead for his repeal,
'Tis not for his sake, but for our avail –
Nay, for the realm's behoof and for the King's.
LANCASTER
Fie Mortimer, dishonour not thyself!
Can this be true, 'twas good to banish him?   245
And is this true, to call him home again?
Such reasons make white black and dark night day.
MORTIMER JUNIOR
My lord of Lancaster, mark the respect.
LANCASTER
In no respect can contraries be true.
ISABELLA
Yet, good my lord, hear what he can allege.   250
WARWICK
All that he speaks is nothing; we are resolved.
MORTIMER JUNIOR
Do you not wish that Gaveston were dead?
PEMBROKE
I would he were.
MORTIMER JUNIOR
Why then, my lord, give me but leave to speak.
MORTIMER SENIOR
But nephew, do not play the sophister.   255

235 *make denial* refuse (to be persuaded)
237 *grant* assent, agree (to Isabella's will)
242 *avail* advantage
243 *behoof* benefit
247 *Such reasons . . . day* proverbial (Tilley B 440)
248 *respect* consideration, special circumstances
251 *nothing* i.e. irrelevant
254 *give me . . . leave* allow me
255 *sophister* philosopher who uses fallacious arguments

MORTIMER JUNIOR
  This which I urge is of a burning zeal
  To mend the King and do our country good.
  Know you not Gaveston hath store of gold,
  Which may in Ireland purchase him such friends
  As he will front the mightiest of us all?   260
  And whereas he shall live and be beloved,
  'Tis hard for us to work his overthrow.
WARWICK
  Mark you but that, my lord of Lancaster.
MORTIMER JUNIOR
  But were he here, detested as he is,
  How easily might some base slave be suborned   265
  To greet his lordship with a poniard,
  And none so much as blame the murderer,
  But rather praise him for that brave attempt,
  And in the chronicle, enrol his name
  For purging of the realm of such a plague.   270
PEMBROKE
  He saith true.
LANCASTER
  Ay, but how chance this was not done before?
MORTIMER JUNIOR
  Because, my lords, it was not thought upon.
  Nay more, when he shall know it lies in us
  To banish him, and then to call him home,   275
  'Twill make him vail the topflag of his pride
  And fear to offend the meanest nobleman.
MORTIMER SENIOR
  But how if he do not, nephew?
MORTIMER JUNIOR
  Then may we with some colour rise in arms,

---

257 *mend* reform
260 *front* confront
261 *whereas* while
262 *work* effect, bring about
265 *suborned* bribed
266 *poniard* dagger
268 *brave* excellent, worthy
       attempt attack, assault
276 *vail* lower
277 *meanest* i.e. of the lowest rank
279 *colour* pretext

For howsoever we have borne it out,   280
'Tis treason to be up against the King.
So shall we have the people of our side,
Which, for his father's sake, lean to the King
But cannot brook a night-grown mushroom –
Such a one as my lord of Cornwall is –   285
Should bear us down of the nobility.
And when the commons and the nobles join,
'Tis not the King can buckler Gaveston;
We'll pull him from the strongest hold he hath.
My lords, if to perform this I be slack,   290
Think me as base a groom as Gaveston.

LANCASTER
On that condition Lancaster will grant.

PEMBROKE
And so will Pembroke.

WARWICK
And I.

MORTIMER SENIOR
And I.   295

MORTIMER JUNIOR
In this I count me highly gratified,
And Mortimer will rest at your command.

ISABELLA
And when this favour Isabel forgets,
Then let her live abandoned and forlorn.

Enter KING EDWARD *mourning*[, *with* BEAUMONT, *the* CLERK
OF THE CROWN, *and attendants*]

But see, in happy time, my lord the King,   300
Having brought the Earl of Cornwall on his way,
Is new returned. This news will glad him much,
Yet not so much as me; I love him more
Than he can Gaveston. Would he loved me

280 *howsoever . . . borne it out* however much we have endured
282 *of* on
284 *mushroom* ed. (mushrump Q1–4) Mushrooms grow overnight; hence a
   metaphor for an upstart, someone who has suddenly acquired reputation and
   influence. Proverbial (Tilley M 1319)
286 i.e. should overwhelm us, members of the nobility
288 *buckler* shield
289 *hold* stronghold, castle
293 sp PEMBROKE ed. (*War.* Q); (*one line in* Q And so will *Penbrooke and I.*)
296 *gratified* pleased, content
299 sd ed.; after line 303 in Q

But half so much, then were I treble blessed.   305

EDWARD

He's gone, and for his absence thus I mourn.
Did never sorrow go so near my heart
As doth the want of my sweet Gaveston;
And could my crown's revènue bring him back,
I would freely give it to his enemies   310
And think I gained, having bought so dear a friend.

ISABELLA

Hark how he harps upon his minion.

EDWARD

My heart is as an anvil unto sorrow,
Which beats upon it like the Cyclops' hammers,
And with the noise turns up my giddy brain   315
And makes me frantic for my Gaveston.
Ah, had some bloodless Fury rose from hell,
And with kingly sceptre struck me dead,
When I was forced to leave my Gaveston.

LANCASTER

Diablo! What passions call you these?   320

ISABELLA

My gracious lord, I come to bring you news.

EDWARD

That you have parlied with your Mortimer.

ISABELLA

That Gaveston, my lord, shall be repealed.

EDWARD

Repealed? The news is too sweet to be true.

ISABELLA

But will you love me if you find it so?   325

EDWARD

If it be so, what will not Edward do?

ISABELLA

For Gaveston, but not for Isabel.

314 *Cyclops* In classical mythology, one-eyed giants employed to forge thunderbolts
     for Jupiter.
315 *up* i.e. upside down
317 *Fury* In classical mythology, the Furies punished wrongdoers, and lived in
     Tartarus (a part of the underworld).
320 *Diablo!* (Spanish) The devil!
     passions (i) lamentations, passionate speeches (ii) intense expressions of love
324 *The news . . . true* proverbial (Tilley N 156)

EDWARD

   For thee, fair Queen, if thou lov'st Gaveston;
   I'll hang a golden tongue about thy neck,
   Seeing thou hast pleaded with so good success.   330

                    [*He embraces her*]

ISABELLA

   No other jewels hang about my neck
   Than these, my lord; nor let me have more wealth
   Than I may fetch from this rich treasury.
   O how a kiss revives poor Isabel.

EDWARD

   Once more receive my hand, and let this be   335
   A second marriage 'twixt thyself and me.

ISABELLA

   And may it prove more happy than the first.
   My gentle lord, bespeak these nobles fair
   That wait attendance for a gracious look,
   And on their knees salute your majesty.   340

                    [*The* NOBLES *kneel*]

EDWARD

   Courageous Lancaster, embrace thy King,
   And as gross vapours perish by the sun,
   Even so let hatred with thy sovereign's smile;
   Live thou with me as my companion.

LANCASTER

   This salutation overjoys my heart.   345

EDWARD

   Warwick, shall be my chiefest counsellor:
   These silver hairs will more adorn my court
   Than gaudy silks or rich embroidery.
   Chide me, sweet Warwick, if I go astray.

WARWICK

   Slay me, my lord, when I offend your grace.   350

EDWARD

   In solemn triumphs and in public shows

---

329 *golden tongue* an item of jewellery. Charlton and Waller cite *The Account of the Lord High Treasurer of Scotland (1488–92)*, 'A grete serpent toung set with gold, perle and precious stanes'.
332 *Than these* i.e. Edward's arms (embracing her)
338 *bespeak* speak to
342 *gross vapours* thick mists, fog
348 *gaudy* ornate
351 *triumphs . . . public shows* pageants, processions, public entertainments

Pembroke shall bear the sword before the King.

PEMBROKE

And with this sword Pembroke will fight for you.

EDWARD

But wherefore walks young Mortimer aside?
Be thou commander of our royal fleet,   355
Or if that lofty office like thee not,
I make thee here Lord Marshal of the realm.

MORTIMER JUNIOR

My lord, I'll marshal so your enemies
As England shall be quiet and you safe.

EDWARD

And as for you, Lord Mortimer of Chirke,   360
Whose great achievements in our foreign war
Deserves no common place nor mean reward,
Be you the general of the levied troops
That now are ready to assail the Scots.

MORTIMER SENIOR

In this your grace hath highly honoured me,   365
For with my nature war doth best agree.

ISABELLA

Now is the King of England rich and strong,
Having the love of his renownèd peers.

EDWARD

Ay, Isabel, ne'er was my heart so light.
Clerk of the Crown, direct our warrant forth   370
For Gaveston to Ireland; Beaumont, fly
As fast as Iris or Jove's Mercury.

BEAUMONT

It shall be done, my gracious lord.

[*Exit* BEAUMONT, *with the* CLERK OF THE CROWN]

EDWARD

Lord Mortimer, we leave you to your charge.
Now let us in and feast it royally   375

---

352 *bear the sword* The sword of state symbolized justice and was carried at the front
   of processions before the monarch.
354 *aside* (i) to one side (ii) apart, away from a group
356 *like* please
360 *Chirke* i.e. Mortimer Senior, whose estate bordered Shropshire and Wales
370 *Clerk of the Crown* an officer of Chancery responsible for framing and issuing
   writs of various sorts in both the House of Lords and the House of Commons
372 *Iris . . . Mercury* In classical mythology, Iris was the rainbow and the messenger
   of the gods; Mercury also served the latter function.

Against our friend the Earl of Cornwall comes.
We'll have a general tilt and tournament,
And then his marriage shall be solemnized;
For wot you not that I have made him sure
Unto our cousin, the Earl of Gloucester's heir?   380
LANCASTER
Such news we hear, my lord.
EDWARD
That day, if not for him, yet for my sake,
Who in the triumph will be challenger,
Spare for no cost; we will requite your love.
WARWICK
In this, or aught, your highness shall command us.   385
EDWARD
Thanks, gentle Warwick; come, let's in and revel.

                    Exeunt [all, except the MORTIMERS]

MORTIMER SENIOR
Nephew, I must to Scotland; thou stayest here.
Leave now to oppose thyself against the King;
Thou seest by nature he is mild and calm,
And seeing his mind so dotes on Gaveston,   390
Let him without controlment have his will.
The mightiest kings have had their minions:
Great Alexander loved Hephaestion;
The conquering Hercules for Hylas wept;
And for Patroclus stern Achilles drooped.   395
And not kings only, but the wisest men:

---

376 *Against* until   377 *tilt* joust
379 *sure* betrothed
380 *Earl of Gloucester's heir* i.e. Lady Margaret de Clare
386 sd ed. (*Manent* Mortimers. Q)
391 *controlment* restraint
393 *Great Alexander . . . Hephaestion* Alexander III of Macedon (356–323 B.C.), the
    celebrated ruler, had an intimate friendship with the military commander
    Hephaestion (d. 325 B.C.).
394 *Hercules* ed. (*Hector* Q). See 1. 143. It seems unlikely that Marlowe would here
    bungle a classical reference which he got right in an earlier scene; and the
    emended line is metrically superior if the word 'conquering' is disyllabic, as it
    usually is in Marlowe's verse.
395 *Achilles* In classical mythology, the Greek warrior who murdered Hector in the
    Trojan Wars following the death of Patroclus, his closest companion. This nar-
    rative is best known in Homer's *Iliad* and was later dramatized by Shakespeare
    in *Troilus and Cressida*, which intimates a homosexual relationship between the
    two warriors.

The Roman Tully loved Octavius,
Grave Socrates, wild Alcibiades.
Then let his grace, whose youth is flexible
And promiseth as much as we can wish,   400
Freely enjoy that vain light-headed Earl,
For riper years will wean him from such toys.

MORTIMER JUNIOR
Uncle, his wanton humour grieves not me,
But this I scorn, that one so basely born
Should by his sovereign's favour grow so pert,   405
And riot it with the treasure of the realm
While soldiers mutiny for want of pay.
He wears a lord's revènue on his back,
And Midas-like he jets it in the court
With base outlandish cullions at his heels,   410
Whose proud fantastic liveries make such show
As if that Proteus, god of shapes, appeared.
I have not seen a dapper jack so brisk;
He wears a short Italian hooded cloak,
Larded with pearl; and in his Tuscan cap   415
A jewel of more value than the crown.
Whiles other walk below, the King and he

397 *Tully* Marcus Tullius Cicero (106–43 B.C.), the Roman statesman. Octavius
    Caesar (63 B.C.–A.D. 14), however, did not have any particular relationship
    with Cicero.
398 *Socrates* Greek philosopher (469–399 B.C.)
    Alcibiades Athenian politician (c. 450–404 B.C.) and pupil of Socrates,
    renowned for his beauty
402 *toys* trifles
408 *wears . . . back* proverbial (Tilley L 452). Cf. *2 Henry VI*, 'She bears a duke's
    revenues on her back' (1.3.83).
409 *Midas* king of Phrygia who was granted the power to turn all that he touched to
    gold. Cf. Ovid's *Metamorphoses*, XI. 92ff
    jets it struts
410 *outlandish* foreign
    cullions low fellows
412 *Proteus* sea god who had the ability to change shape. Cf. Ovid's *Metamorphoses*,
    VIII. 730–7.
413 *dapper jack* fashionable gentleman
    brisk smartly dressed
414–15 Gaveston's taste in clothes serves to emphasize his homosexuality, thought
    by the Elizabethans to be a particularly Italian vice.
415 *Larded* excessively decorated
    Tuscan cap a fashionable hat from Tuscany, made from finely woven straw
417 *other* others

From out a window laugh at such as we,
And flout our train and jest at our attire.
Uncle, 'tis this that makes me impatient.   420
MORTIMER SENIOR
But nephew, now you see the King is changed.
MORTIMER JUNIOR
Then so am I, and live to do him service;
But whiles I have a sword, a hand, a heart,
I will not yield to any such upstart.
You know my mind. Come, uncle, let's away.   *Exeunt* 425

[Scene 5]

Enter SPENCER [JUNIOR] *and* BALDOCK

BALDOCK
Spencer,
Seeing that our lord th' Earl of Gloucester's dead,
Which of the nobles dost thou mean to serve?
SPENCER JUNIOR
Not Mortimer, nor any of his side,
Because the King and he are enemies.   5
Baldock, learn this of me: a factious lord
Shall hardly do himself good, much less us;
But he that hath the favour of a king
May with one word advance us while we live.
The liberal Earl of Cornwall is the man   10
On whose good fortune Spencer's hope depends.
BALDOCK
What, mean you then to be his follower?
SPENCER JUNIOR
No, his companion; for he loves me well
And would have once preferred me to the King.
BALDOCK
But he is banished; there's small hope of him.   15

---

419 *flout* mock
     train attendants

1–2 ed. (*Spencer,* seeing . . . Glo- / sters dead, Q)
6 *factious* seditious
10 *liberal* (i) one who displays the qualities of a gentleman (ii) one who behaves
      licentiously
12 *follower* retainer
14 *preferred . . . to* (i) recommended to (ii) favoured more than (i.e. sexually)

SPENCER JUNIOR
  Ay, for a while; but, Baldock, mark the end:
  A friend of mine told me in secrecy
  That he's repealed and sent for back again;
  And even now, a post came from the court
  With letters to our lady from the King,   20
  And as she read, she smiled, which makes me think
  It is about her lover, Gaveston.
BALDOCK
  'Tis like enough, for since he was exiled,
  She neither walks abroad nor comes in sight.
  But I had thought the match had been broke off   25
  And that his banishment had changed her mind.
SPENCER JUNIOR
  Our lady's first love is not wavering;
  My life for thine, she will have Gaveston.
BALDOCK
  Then hope I by her means to be preferred,
  Having read unto her since she was a child.   30
SPENCER JUNIOR
  Then, Baldock, you must cast the scholar off
  And learn to court it like a gentleman.
  'Tis not a black coat and a little band,
  A velvet-caped cloak, faced before with serge,
  And smelling to a nosegay all the day,   35
  Or holding of a napkin in your hand,

---

16 *end* conclusion
20 *our lady* i.e. Margaret de Clare, daughter of the dead Earl of Gloucester
28 *My life . . . thine* proverbial (Dent L 260.1)
30 *Having read unto her* Baldock, an Oxford scholar, is portrayed as Margaret de Clare's tutor.
31 *cast the scholar off* i.e. cease to behave like an academic
32 *court it* behave like a courtier
33–4 Spencer Junior 'gives a thumbnail sketch of the typical poor scholar who failed to achieve academic preferment and was compelled to take up duties in a nobleman's household, tutoring the children and acting as domestic chaplain' (Gill). Many editors cite John Earle's 'A young raw Preacher' in his *Micro-cosmographie* (1628), 'His fashion and demure habit gets him in with some town-precisian, and makes him a guest on Friday nights. You shall know him by his narrow veluet cape, and serge facing, and his ruffe, next his haire, the shortest thing about him' (Sig. B4ᵛ).
33 *black coat . . . little band* subfusc or academic dress
34 *faced* trimmed, patched
   serge cheap woollen material
35 *nosegay* posy, bunch of flowers

Or saying a long grace at a table's end,
Or making low legs to a nobleman,
Or looking downward, with your eyelids close,
And saying, 'Truly, an't may please your honour',   40
Can get you any favour with great men.
You must be proud, bold, pleasant, resolute,
And now and then, stab, as occasion serves.

BALDOCK
Spencer, thou knowest I hate such formal toys,
And use them but of mere hypocrisy.   45
Mine old lord, whiles he lived, was so precise
That he would take exceptions at my buttons,
And, being like pins' heads, blame me for the bigness,
Which made me curate-like in mine attire,
Though inwardly licentious enough   50
And apt for any kind of villainy.
I am none of these common pedants, I,
That cannot speak without 'propterea quod'.

SPENCER JUNIOR
But one of those that saith 'quandoquidem'
And hath a special gift to form a verb.   55

BALDOCK
Leave off this jesting – here my lady comes.

[*They withdraw*]

37 *table's end* the bottom end of the table (below the salt) which signified the lowest position of social status
38 *low legs* deferential, obeisant bowing
40 *an't* if it
42 *pleasant* jocular
43 *stab* with pun on sexual thrusting
44 *formal toys* trivial formalities, conventions
46 *old* former   *whiles* while   *precise* punctilious, puritanical
47 *take exceptions at* find fault with
50 *licentious* (i) unrestrained, indecorous (ii) given to sexual licence
51 *apt* ready, prepared
52 *common* ordinary
   pedants ed. (pendants Q; pedants Q2–4) schoolmasters, tutors
53, 54 *propterea quod, quandoquidem* Even though both expressions mean 'because',
the former phrase (as suggested by Briggs) is prosaic and less refined than the
verse of 'quandoquidem'; perhaps varsity humour is implied. Arguably, their use
of Latin ridicules the affected rhetoric of scholarship.
55 *to form* to conjugate
56 *off* ed. (of Q)
56 sd 1 *They withdraw* They move to the side of the stage, and Lady Margaret is
apparently unaware of their presence, watching and overhearing her.

Enter the LADY [MARGARET DE CLARE, *with letters*]

LADY MARGARET
The grief for his exile was not so much
As is the joy of his returning home.
This letter came from my sweet Gaveston.

[*She reads the letter*]

What needst thou love, thus to excuse thyself?   60
I know thou couldst not come and visit me.
'I will not long be from thee, though I die':
This argues the entire love of my lord;
'When I forsake thee, death seize on my heart.'
But rest thee here where Gaveston shall sleep.   65

[*She places the letter in her bosom*]

Now to the letter of my lord the King.

[*She reads another letter*]

He wills me to repair unto the court
And meet my Gaveston. Why do I stay,
Seeing that he talks thus of my marriage-day?
Who's there? Baldock?   70

[BALDOCK *and* SPENCER JUNIOR *come forward*]

See that my coach be ready; I must hence.
BALDOCK
It shall be done, madam.
LADY MARGARET
And meet me at the park pale presently.   *Exit* [BALDOCK]
Spencer, stay you and bear me company,
For I have joyful news to tell thee of.   75
My lord of Cornwall is a-coming over
And will be at the court as soon as we.
SPENCER JUNIOR
I knew the King would have him home again.
LADY MARGARET
If all things sort out, as I hope they will,

---

67 *repair* come
71 *coach* In fact, coaches were not ordinarily used in England until after 1564.
73 *park pale* the fencing of an estate or park
       presently directly
73 sd ed. (*Exit.* Q after 'madam', line 72)
74 *bear me company* i.e. keep me company

Thy service, Spencer, shall be thought upon.   80
SPENCER JUNIOR
I humbly thank your ladyship.
LADY MARGARET
Come, lead the way; I long till I am there.   [*Exeunt*]

[Scene 6]

Enter EDWARD, [ISABELLA] *the Queen*, LANCASTER, MORTIMER
[JUNIOR], WARWICK, PEMBROKE, KENT, *attendants*

EDWARD
The wind is good, I wonder why he stays.
I fear me he is wrecked upon the sea.
ISABELLA
Look, Lancaster, how passionate he is,
And still his mind runs on his minion.
LANCASTER
My lord –   5
EDWARD
How now, what news? Is Gaveston arrived?
MORTIMER JUNIOR
Nothing but Gaveston! What means your grace?
You have matters of more weight to think upon;
The King of France sets foot in Normandy.
EDWARD
A trifle! We'll expel him when we please.   10
But tell me, Mortimer, what's thy device
Against the stately triumph we decreed?
MORTIMER JUNIOR
A homely one, my lord, not worth the telling.
EDWARD
Prithee let me know it.
MORTIMER JUNIOR
But seeing you are so desirous, thus it is: 15

82 *long* am restless

3 *passionate* grief-stricken, sorrowful
4 *runs on* is pre
9 Normandy was part of English crown territory; cf. 11. 64.
11 *device* an heraldic emblem (painted on a shield)
12 *Against* prepared for
    triumph public entertainment, pageant, festival
13 *homely* plain, not ostentatious

A lofty cedar tree fair flourishing,
On whose top branches kingly eagles perch,
And by the bark a canker creeps me up
And gets unto the highest bough of all;
The motto: *Æque tandem.*   20
EDWARD
And what is yours, my lord of Lancaster?
LANCASTER
My lord, mine's more obscure than Mortimer's:
Pliny reports there is a flying fish
Which all the other fishes deadly hate,
And therefore, being pursued, it takes the air;   25
No sooner is it up, but there's a fowl
That seizeth it. This fish, my lord, I bear;
The motto this: *Undique mors est.*
EDWARD
Proud Mortimer! Ungentle Lancaster!
Is this the love you bear your sovereign?   30
Is this the fruit your reconcilement bears?
Can you in words make show of amity,
And in your shields display your rancorous minds?
What call you this but private libelling
Against the Earl of Cornwall and my brother?   35
ISABELLA
Sweet husband, be content; they all love you.
EDWARD
They love me not that hate my Gaveston.

16 *lofty* A latent double meaning implies Gaveston's arrogance.
   cedar tree symbol of the structure of society with the King represented by the
   highest bough
18 *canker* worm which consumes plants
   creeps me up creeps up
20 *Æque tandem* (Latin) Equal in height. Mortimer Junior is suggesting that
   Gaveston is the canker which is infecting the state, moving from the base (i.e.
   the commons) to the top (i.e. the nobility).
21 *yours* i.e. the device on Lancaster's shield
22 *obscure* hard to interpret
23 *Pliny* Gaius Plinius Secundus or Pliny the Elder (A.D. 23/4–79), Roman scholar
   and naturalist best known for his *Naturalis Historia* (A.D. 77)
28 *Undique mors est* (Latin) Death is on all sides.
31 *reconcilement* reconciliation
34 *libelling* Rowland points out that this is an anachronism: 'libel in the sense of a
   defamatory document or statement was a sixteenth-century development'.
35 *my brother* i.e. Gaveston

I am that cedar; shake me not too much.
And you the eagles; soar ye ne'er so high,
I have the jesses that will pull you down,   40
And '*Æque tandem*' shall that canker cry
Unto the proudest peer of Britainy.
Though thou compar'st him to a flying fish,
And threatenest death whether he rise or fall,
'Tis not the hugest monster of the sea   45
Nor foulest harpy that shall swallow him.

MORTIMER JUNIOR
[*To the* NOBLES] If in his absence thus he favours him,
What will he do whenas he shall be present?

Enter GAVESTON

LANCASTER
That shall we see: look where his lordship comes.

EDWARD
My Gaveston!   50
Welcome to Tynemouth, welcome to thy friend.
Thy absence made me droop and pine away;
For as the lovers of fair Danaë,
When she was locked up in a brazen tower,
Desired her more and waxed outrageous,   55
So did it sure with me; and now thy sight
Is sweeter far than was thy parting hence
Bitter and irksome to my sobbing heart.

GAVESTON
Sweet lord and King, your speech preventeth mine,

40 *jesses* (gresses Q) straps which were fastened to the legs of hawks
42 *Britainy* Britain (England and Scotland)
43–6 Edward draws upon the images of the flying fish and the fowl (from
  Lancaster's description of his device) and exaggerates them in order to undermine the verbal assaults of the two nobles.
46 *harpy* in classical mythology, bird-like creatures with female faces and breasts,
  which stole food and harassed Phineus, the blind King of Thrace, when he
  entertained the Argonauts
48 *whenas* when
48 sd ed.; after line 49 in Q
53 *Danaë* In classical mythology, she was incarcerated by her father in a bronze
  tower after an oracle prophesied that her son would murder him; Jupiter then
  visited her in a shower of gold and she conceived the hero Perseus.
55 *waxed* grew
  outrageous unrestrained (four syllables)
59 *preventeth* anticipates

Yet have I words left to express my joy: 60
The shepherd nipped with biting winter's rage
Frolics not more to see the painted spring
Than I do to behold your majesty.
EDWARD
Will none of you salute my Gaveston?
LANCASTER
Salute him? Yes! Welcome, Lord Chamberlain.   65
MORTIMER JUNIOR
Welcome is the good Earl of Cornwall.
WARWICK
Welcome, Lord Governor of the Isle of Man.
PEMBROKE
Welcome, Master Secretary.
KENT
Brother, do you hear them?
EDWARD
Still will these earls and barons use me thus!   70
GAVESTON
My lord, I cannot brook these injuries.
ISABELLA
[*Aside*] Ay me, poor soul, when these begin to jar.
EDWARD
Return it to their throats; I'll be thy warrant.
GAVESTON
Base leaden earls that glory in your birth,
Go sit at home and eat your tenants' beef,   75
And come not here to scoff at Gaveston,
Whose mounting thoughts did never creep so low
As to bestow a look on such as you.

62 *painted* colourful, decorated with flowers
70 *use* behave towards, treat
72 *jar* quarrel, wrangle
73 *Return . . . throats* i.e. reject their abuse, 'give them the lie' (a provocative act,
   normally a formal challenge to a duel); cf. Shakespeare, *Titus Andronicus*,
   2.1.53–6
   warrant document of authorization
74 *Base leaden* Gaveston likens the nobles to the dullness of cheap alloy coins, with
   a latent pun on the name of a gold coin, a 'noble'.
75 *eat . . . beef* an insult, implying that the nobles are 'beef-witted' (stupid, brain-
   less). Forker suggests that Frenchmen such as Gaveston regarded the English as
   great eaters of beef.

LANCASTER
Yet I disdain not to do this for you.   [*Draws his sword*]
EDWARD
Treason, treason! Where's the traitor?
PEMBROKE [*indicating* GAVESTON]   Here, here!   80
EDWARD
Convey hence Gaveston; they'll murder him.
GAVESTON
The life of thee shall salve this foul disgrace.
MORTIMER JUNIOR
Villain, thy life, unless I miss mine aim.

[*He wounds* GAVESTON]

ISABELLA
Ah, furious Mortimer, what hast thou done?
MORTIMER JUNIOR
No more than I would answer were he slain.   85

[*Exit* GAVESTON, *attended*]

EDWARD
Yes, more than thou canst answer, though he live;
Dear shall you both aby this riotous deed.
Out of my presence! Come not near the court.
MORTIMER JUNIOR
I'll not be barred the court for Gaveston.
LANCASTER
We'll hale him by the ears unto the block.   90
EDWARD
Look to your own heads; his is sure enough.
WARWICK
Look to your own crown, if you back him thus.
KENT
Warwick, these words do ill beseem thy years.

---

79   sd: It was an offence to brandish weapons in the King's presence.
80–1 ed. Q erroneously prints Edward's line and speech prefix as part of
      Pembroke's dialogue. (Heere here King: conuey . . . thaile / murder him.)
82   *salve* atone, remedy (vindication is implied)
85   *answer* answer for
87   *both* i.e. Mortimer Junior and Lancaster
      aby pay for, atone   *riotous* wanton, amoral
90   *hale* drag, pull (forcibly)
91   *sure* safe
93   *ill beseem . . . years* i.e. you should display greater wisdom and prudence,
      considering your age

EDWARD
Nay, all of them conspire to cross me thus;
But if I live, I'll tread upon their heads   95
That think with high looks thus to tread me down.
Come, Edmund, let's away and levy men;
'Tis war that must abate these barons' pride.

Exit [EDWARD] *the King*[, *with* ISABELLA *and* KENT]

WARWICK
Let's to our castles, for the King is moved.
MORTIMER JUNIOR
Moved may he be and perish in his wrath.   100
LANCASTER
Cousin, it is no dealing with him now.
He means to make us stoop by force of arms,
And therefore let us jointly here protest
To prosecute that Gaveston to the death.
MORTIMER JUNIOR
By heaven, the abject villain shall not live.   105
WARWICK
I'll have his blood or die in seeking it.
PEMBROKE
The like oath Pembroke takes.
LANCASTER   And so doth Lancaster.
Now send our heralds to defy the King
And make the people swear to put him down.

Enter a POST

MORTIMER JUNIOR
Letters? From whence?   110
POST
From Scotland, my lord.

94 *cross* obstruct, thwart
101 *Cousin* used more broadly than in modern English, to denote a variety of kinship
and other associations
  it is there is
102 *stoop* submit
103 *protest* vow
104 *prosecute* pursue
105 *abject* most contemptible, servile
108 *heralds* messengers or officials used in time of war to carry messages to the enemy
109 sd POST messenger
111 sp POST ed. (*Messen.* Q)

LANCASTER
Why how now, cousin, how fares all our friends?
MORTIMER JUNIOR
[*Reading a letter*] My uncle's taken prisoner by the Scots.
LANCASTER
We'll have him ransomed, man; be of good cheer.
MORTIMER JUNIOR
They rate his ransom at five thousand pound.   115
Who should defray the money but the King,
Seeing he is taken prisoner in his wars?
I'll to the King.
LANCASTER
Do cousin, and I'll bear thee company.
WARWICK
Meantime, my lord of Pembroke and myself   120
Will to Newcastle here and gather head.
MORTIMER JUNIOR
About it then, and we will follow you.
LANCASTER
Be resolute and full of secrecy.
WARWICK
I warrant you.

[*Exeunt all but* MORTIMER JUNIOR *and* LANCASTER]

MORTIMER JUNIOR
Cousin, an if he will not ransom him,   125
I'll thunder such a peal into his ears
As never subject did unto his king.
LANCASTER
Content; I'll bear my part. Holla! Who's there?

[*Enter a* GUARD]

MORTIMER JUNIOR
Ay, marry, such a guard as this doth well.
LANCASTER
Lead on the way.
GUARD   Whither will your lordships?   130

116 *defray* pay for, settle the payment
121 *gather head* raise forces
123 *resolute* determined
124 *warrant* give assurance
128 *Content* agreed
129 *marry* to be sure (contracted form of the affirmation 'By Mary')

MORTIMER JUNIOR
Whither else but to the King?
GUARD
His highness is disposed to be alone.
LANCASTER
Why, so he may, but we will speak to him.
GUARD
You may not in, my lord.
MORTIMER JUNIOR
May we not?   135

[*Enter* EDWARD *and* KENT]

EDWARD
How now, what noise is this?
Who have we there? Is't you?

[*He makes to exit, ignoring* MORTIMER JUNIOR *and* LANCASTER]

MORTIMER JUNIOR
Nay, stay, my lord; I come to bring you news:
Mine uncle's taken prisoner by the Scots.
EDWARD
Then ransom him.   140
LANCASTER
'Twas in your wars: you should ransom him.
MORTIMER JUNIOR
And you shall ransom him, or else –
KENT
What, Mortimer, you will not threaten him?
EDWARD
Quiet yourself; you shall have the broad seal
To gather for him thoroughout the realm.   145
LANCASTER
Your minion Gaveston hath taught you this.
MORTIMER JUNIOR
My lord, the family of the Mortimers
Are not so poor but, would they sell their land,
Would levy men enough to anger you.

---

134 *in* i.e. enter the King's chamber
144 *broad seal* letters patent giving the bearer the right to raise money for a specific
   purpose without being prosecuted for begging. Edward's offer insultingly implies that Mortimer Junior is impoverished.
145 *gather* collect money
   thoroughout throughout

We never beg, but use such prayers as these.   150

[*He puts his hand on the hilt of his sword*]

EDWARD
Shall I still be haunted thus?
MORTIMER JUNIOR
Nay, now you are here alone, I'll speak my mind.
LANCASTER
And so will I; and then, my lord, farewell.
MORTIMER JUNIOR
The idle triumphs, masques, lascivious shows,
And prodigal gifts bestowed on Gaveston   155
Have drawn thy treasure dry and made thee weak;
The murmuring commons overstretchèd hath.
LANCASTER
Look for rebellion, look to be deposed:
Thy garrisons are beaten out of France,
And, lame and poor, lie groaning at the gates;   160
The wild O'Neill, with swarms of Irish kerns,
Lives uncontrolled within the English pale;
Unto the walls of York the Scots made road
And, unresisted, drave away rich spoils.
MORTIMER JUNIOR
The haughty Dane commands the narrow seas,   165
While in the harbour ride thy ships unrigged.

151 *haunted* persistently molested
154 *idle* vain, worthless
155 *prodigal* lavish, extravagant
156 *drawn* emptied, drained
    treasure treasury
157 *murmuring* discontented, disgruntled
    commons the common people
    overstretchèd i.e. created an intolerable strain
161 *The . . . O'Neill* prominent Ulster clan chieftain, not mentioned in the sources.
    In 1592, the title was contested; it was conferred on Hugh O'Neill, 2nd Earl of
    Tyrone, in May 1593.
    Irish kerns footsoldiers, commonly recruited from the poorer class of the 'wild
    Irish'
162 *English pale* an area of land around Dublin established for the protection of
    English settlers
163 *made road* raided
164 *drave* drove
    spoils plunder, booty
165 *the narrow seas* the English Channel
166 *ride* lie at anchor
    unrigged without their rigging

LANCASTER
What foreign prince sends thee ambassadors?
MORTIMER JUNIOR
Who loves thee but a sort of flatterers?
LANCASTER
Thy gentle Queen, sole sister to Valois,
Complains that thou hast left her all forlorn.   170
MORTIMER JUNIOR
Thy court is naked, being bereft of those
That makes a king seem glorious to the world –
I mean the peers whom thou shouldst dearly love.
Libels are cast again thee in the street,
Ballads and rhymes made of thy overthrow.   175
LANCASTER
The northern borderers, seeing their houses burnt,
Their wives and children slain, run up and down
Cursing the name of thee and Gaveston.
MORTIMER JUNIOR
When wert thou in the field with banner spread?
But once! And then thy soldiers marched like players,   180
With garish robes, not armour; and thyself,
Bedaubed with gold, rode laughing at the rest,
Nodding and shaking of thy spangled crest
Where women's favours hung like labels down.
LANCASTER
And thereof came it that the fleering Scots,   185
To England's high disgrace, have made this jig:

168 *sort* group
169 *Valois* i.e. Philip, King of France (family name)
170 *forlorn* desolate, abandoned
171 *naked* destitute
172 *seem* appear
174 *Libels* subversive pamphlets
     again against
175 *Ballads and rhymes* In Elizabethan England, these were the cheapest and most
     demotic form of literature, costing one penny.
176 *their* ed. (the Q)
180 *players* actors
183 *crest* the plume or decoration on the top of a helmet
184 *favours* tokens of affection or keepsakes (gloves, scarves) given by ladies to
     knights and worn either in battle or in a tournament
     labels slips of paper or parchment for attaching seals to documents
185 *fleering* sneering, jeering
186 *jig* insulting song or ballad

'Maids of England, sore may you mourn,
For your lemans you have lost at Bannockburn.
    With a heave and a ho.
What weeneth the King of England,   190
    So soon to have won Scotland?
    With a rumbelow.'
MORTIMER JUNIOR
Wigmore shall fly, to set my uncle free.
LANCASTER
And when 'tis gone, our swords shall purchase more.
If ye be moved, revenge it as you can;   195
Look next to see us with our ensigns spread.

            Exeunt NOBLES [LANCASTER *and* MORTIMER JUNIOR]

EDWARD
My swelling heart for very anger breaks!
How oft have I been baited by these peers
And dare not be revenged, for their power is great?
Yet, shall the crowing of these cockerels   200
Affright a lion? Edward, unfold thy paws
And let their lives' blood slake thy fury's hunger.
If I be cruel and grow tyrannous,
Now let them thank themselves and rue too late.
KENT
My lord, I see your love to Gaveston   205
Will be the ruin of the realm and you,
For now the wrathful nobles threaten wars;
And therefore, brother, banish him forever.
EDWARD
Art thou an enemy to my Gaveston?
KENT
Ay, and it grieves me that I favoured him.   210
EDWARD
Traitor, be gone; whine thou with Mortimer.

188 *lemans* sweethearts
    Bannockburn The battle of Bannockburn (24 June 1314) ended in the defeat of
    Edward's forces following an attempt to secure Stirling Castle from the Scots.
    The Q spelling, 'Bannocksborne', emphasizes the rhyme.
190 *weeneth* hopes, expects
192 *rumbelow* meaningless refrain which maintains the rhyme of the song
193 *Wigmore* Wigmore Castle (Mortimer Junior's Herefordshire estate)
    shall fly i.e. shall be sold
194 *purchase* earn, acquire
196 *ensigns* banners (displayed by each side in battle)
200-1 *cockerels . . . lion* The lion was, in fact, proverbially afraid of the cock's crow-
    ing; see *MLN* 50 (1935), 352-4.

KENT
 So will I, rather than with Gaveston.
EDWARD
 Out of my sight, and trouble me no more.
KENT
 No marvel though thou scorn thy noble peers,
 When I thy brother am rejected thus.   215
EDWARD
 Away!   *Exit* [KENT]
 Poor Gaveston, that hast no friend but me.
 Do what they can, we'll live in Tynemouth here,
 And, so I walk with him about the walls,
 What care I though the earls begirt us round?   220

   Enter [ISABELLA] *the Queen, three ladies* [MARGARET DE
   CLARE *with two ladies in waiting,* GAVESTON], BALDOCK,
                and SPENCER [JUNIOR]

 Here comes she that's cause of all these jars.
ISABELLA
 My lord, 'tis thought the earls are up in arms.
EDWARD
 Ay, and 'tis likewise thought you favour him.
ISABELLA
 Thus do you still suspect me without cause.
LADY MARGARET
 Sweet uncle, speak more kindly to the Queen.   225
GAVESTON [*Aside to* EDWARD]
 My lord, dissemble with her, speak her fair.
EDWARD
 Pardon me, sweet, I forgot myself.
ISABELLA
 Your pardon is quickly got of Isabel.
EDWARD
 The younger Mortimer is grown so brave
 That to my face he threatens civil wars.   230
GAVESTON
 Why do you not commit him to the Tower?

216–17 ed. (*one line in* Q)
220 *begirt* surround, enclose
220 sd ed. (after 221 in Q: *Enter the Queene, Ladies 3, Baldock, / and Spencer.*)
223 *him* Mortimer Junior; Edward is more preoccupied with personal than political
    betrayal
226 *fair* courteously
229 *brave* defiant, impertinent

EDWARD
I dare not, for the people love him well.
GAVESTON
Why then, we'll have him privily made away.
EDWARD
Would Lancaster and he had both caroused
A bowl of poison to each other's health. 235
But let them go, and tell me what are these?
LADY MARGARET
Two of my father's servants whilst he lived;
May't please your grace to entertain them now.
EDWARD
Tell me, where wast thou born? What is thine arms?
BALDOCK
My name is Baldock, and my gentry 240
I fetched from Oxford, not from heraldry.
EDWARD
The fitter art thou, Baldock, for my turn;
Wait on me, and I'll see thou shalt not want.
BALDOCK
I humbly thank your majesty.
EDWARD
Knowest thou him, Gaveston?
GAVESTON   Ay, my lord. 245
His name is Spencer; he is well allied.
For my sake let him wait upon your grace;
Scarce shall you find a man of more desert.
EDWARD
Then, Spencer, wait upon me; for his sake
I'll grace thee with a higher style ere long. 250
SPENCER JUNIOR
    No greater titles happen unto me

---

233 *privily made away* secretly murdered   234 *caroused* quaffed
235 *health* well-being, prosperity (with ironic pun on physical health)
236 *let them go* i.e. enough talk of them (Forker)
238 *entertain* take into service, employ
239 ed. (Tell . . . borne? / VVhat . . . armes? Q)   *arms* coat of arms
240 *gentry* rank (of a gentleman)
241 *fetched . . . Oxford* The status of a gentleman could be acquired through having
    been educated at Oxford.
    heraldry heraldic title, rank
245–6 ed. (*Edw.* Knowest . . . *Gaueston?* / *Gau.* I . . . alied, Q)
246 *well allied* well connected, of good birth
250 *style* title, status
251 *happen unto me* i.e. could befall me

Than to be favoured of your majesty.

EDWARD [*To* LADY MARGARET]

Cousin, this day shall be your marriage feast.
And, Gaveston, think that I love thee well
To wed thee to our niece, the only heir   255
Unto the Earl of Gloucester late deceased.

GAVESTON

I know, my lord, many will stomach me,
But I respect neither their love nor hate.

EDWARD

The headstrong barons shall not limit me;
He that I list to favour shall be great.   260
Come, let's away; and when the marriage ends,
Have at the rebels and their complices.   *Exeunt*

[Scene 7]

Enter LANCASTER, MORTIMER [JUNIOR], WARWICK,
PEMBROKE, KENT

KENT

My lords, of love to this our native land
I come to join with you and leave the King;
And in your quarrel and the realm's behoof
Will be the first that shall adventure life.

· LANCASTER

I fear me you are sent of policy   5
To undermine us with a show of love.

WARWICK

He is your brother; therefore have we cause
To cast the worst and doubt of your revolt.

KENT

Mine honour shall be hostage of my truth;
If that will not suffice, farewell, my lords.   10

MORTIMER JUNIOR

Stay, Edmund; never was Plantagenet
False of his word, and therefore trust we thee.

252 *of* by   253 *Cousin* Cf. 101 n. above.
257 *stomach* resent
260 *list* choose
262 *Have at* attack   *complices* confederates

3 *behoof* benefit   4 *adventure* risk
5 *of policy* i.e. out of deceit, under false pretences
8 *cast* reckon, fear   *doubt of* suspect

PEMBROKE
    But what's the reason you should leave him now?
KENT
    I have informed the Earl of Lancaster.
LANCASTER
    And it sufficeth. Now, my lords, know this,   15
    That Gaveston is secretly arrived,
    And here in Tynemouth frolics with the King.
    Let us with these our followers scale the walls,
    And suddenly surprise them unawares.
MORTIMER JUNIOR
    I'll give the onset.
WARWICK   And I'll follow thee.   20
MORTIMER JUNIOR
    This tattered ensign of my ancestors,
    Which swept the desert shore of that dead sea
    Whereof we got the name of Mortimer,
    Will I advance upon these castle walls.
    Drums strike alarum! Raise them from their sport,   25
    And ring aloud the knell of Gaveston.   *[Alarums]*
LANCASTER
    None be so hardy as to touch the King;
    But neither spare you Gaveston nor his friends.   *Exeunt*

[Scene 8]

Enter [EDWARD] *the King and* SPENCER [JUNIOR; *from
another door enter*] *to them* GAVESTON[, *unseen by*
EDWARD *and* SPENCER JUNIOR; *with* ISABELLA, LADY
MARGARET DE CLARE, *and attendants*]

EDWARD
    O tell me, Spencer, where is Gaveston?
SPENCER JUNIOR
    I fear me he is slain, my gracious lord.

17 *frolics* makes merry (the verb also has sexual connotations)
22–3 The Mortimers came from Mortemer in Normandy, and were not, as
    Marlowe suggests, connected with the Crusades and the Dead Sea (*Mortuum
    Mare* in Latin).
24 *these* ed. (this Q) The Q reading could make sense if 'castle' is taken to be a
    genitive with silent final -*s*.
25 *alarum* call to arms, battle-cry
    sport idle pastimes, amusements
27 *hardy* bold, reckless

() sd ed. (*Enter the king and Spencer, to them / Gaueston, &c.* Q)

EDWARD
No, here he comes! Now let them spoil and kill.
Fly, fly, my lords; the earls have got the hold.
Take shipping and away to Scarborough;   5
Spencer and I will post away by land.
GAVESTON
O stay, my lord; they will not injure you.
EDWARD
I will not trust them, Gaveston. Away!
GAVESTON
Farewell, my lord.
EDWARD
Lady, farewell.   10
LADY MARGARET
Farewell, sweet uncle, till we meet again.
EDWARD
Farewell, sweet Gaveston, and farewell, niece.
ISABELLA
No farewell to poor Isabel, thy Queen?
EDWARD
Yes, yes - for Mortimer, your lover's sake.

Exeunt [all, except] ISABELLA

ISABELLA
Heavens can witness, I love none but you.   15
From my embracements thus he breaks away;
O that mine arms could close this isle about,
That I might pull him to me where I would,
Or that these tears that drizzle from mine eyes
Had power to mollify his stony heart   20
That when I had him we might never part.

Enter the Barons [LANCASTER, WARWICK, MORTIMER JUNIOR].
                                              Alarums

LANCASTER
I wonder how he 'scaped?
MORTIMER JUNIOR
Who's this, the Queen?

3 *spoil* plunder, destroy
4 *hold* fortress
6 *post* go with speed (by horse)
14 sd ed. (*Exeunt omnes, manet Isabella.* Q)
21 sd ed. (*Enter the Barons alarums.* Q)

ISABELLA
  Ay, Mortimer, the miserable Queen,
  Whose pining heart, her inward sighs have blasted,   25
  And body with continual mourning wasted.
  These hands are tired with haling of my lord
  From Gaveston, from wicked Gaveston,
  And all in vain; for when I speak him fair,
  He turns away and smiles upon his minion.   30
MORTIMER JUNIOR
  Cease to lament, and tell us where's the King?
ISABELLA
  What would you with the King? Is't him you seek?
LANCASTER
  No, madam, but that cursèd Gaveston.
  Far be it from the thought of Lancaster
  To offer violence to his sovereign.   35
  We would but rid the realm of Gaveston;
  Tell us where he remains, and he shall die.
ISABELLA
  He's gone by water unto Scarborough.
  Pursue him quickly and he cannot 'scape;
  The King hath left him, and his train is small.   40
WARWICK
  Forslow no time, sweet Lancaster; let's march.
MORTIMER JUNIOR
  How comes it that the King and he is parted?
ISABELLA
  That this your army, going several ways,
  Might be of lesser force, and with the power
  That he intendeth presently to raise   45
  Be easily suppressed; and therefore be gone.
MORTIMER JUNIOR
  Here in the river rides a Flemish hoy;
  Let's all aboard and follow him amain.
LANCASTER
  The wind that bears him hence will fill our sails.
  Come, come aboard – 'tis but an hour's sailing.   50
MORTIMER JUNIOR
  Madam, stay you within this castle here.

---

27 *haling* dragging (forcibly)
40 *train* retinue
41 *Forslow* waste
47 *Flemish hoy* small fishing ship used by the Flemings in the North Sea
48 *amain* with all speed

ISABELLA
No, Mortimer, I'll to my lord the King.
MORTIMER JUNIOR
Nay, rather sail with us to Scarborough.
ISABELLA
You know the King is so suspicious,
As if he hear I have but talked with you,   55
Mine honour will be called in question;
And therefore, gentle Mortimer, be gone.
MORTIMER JUNIOR
Madam, I cannot stay to answer you;
But think of Mortimer as he deserves.

[*Exeunt* LANCASTER, WARWICK, *and* MORTIMER JUNIOR]

ISABELLA
So well hast thou deserved, sweet Mortimer,   60
As Isabel could live with thee forever.
In vain I look for love at Edward's hand,
Whose eyes are fixed on none but Gaveston.
Yet once more I'll importune him with prayers;
If he be strange and not regard my words,   65
My son and I will over into France,
And to the King, my brother, there complain
How Gaveston hath robbed me of his love.
But yet I hope my sorrows will have end
And Gaveston this blessèd day be slain.   [*Exit*]   70

[Scene 9]

Enter GAVESTON *pursued*

GAVESTON
Yet, lusty lords, I have escaped your hands,
Your threats, your 'larums, and your hot pursuits;
And though divorcèd from King Edward's eyes,
Yet liveth Piers of Gaveston unsurprised,
Breathing, in hope (*malgrado* all your beards   5

---

65 *strange* estranged, unresponsive
70 sd (*Exeunt* Q)

1 *lusty* arrogant, insolent
2 *'larums* battle-cries
4 *unsurprised* unambushed (and therefore uncaptured)
5 *malgrado . . . beards* in defiance or direct opposition to your purposes; proverbial
    (Tilley S 764)

That muster rebels thus against your King)
To see his royal sovereign once again.

Enter the NOBLES [LANCASTER, WARWICK, PEMBROKE,
MORTIMER JUNIOR, *with soldiers*, JAMES, HORSE-BOY, *and*
PEMBROKE'S MEN]

WARWICK
Upon him, soldiers! Take away his weapons.
MORTIMER JUNIOR
Thou proud disturber of thy country's peace,
Corrupter of thy King, cause of these broils,   10
Base flatterer, yield! And were it not for shame –
Shame and dishonour to a soldier's name –
Upon my weapon's point here shouldst thou fall,
And welter in thy gore.
LANCASTER   Monster of men,
That, like the Greekish strumpet, trained to arms   15
And bloody wars so many valiant knights,
Look for no other fortune, wretch, than death;
King Edward is not here to buckler thee.
WARWICK
Lancaster, why talk'st thou to the slave?
Go, soldiers, take him hence; for by my sword,   20
His head shall off. Gaveston, short warning
Shall serve thy turn; it is our country's cause
That here severely we will execute
Upon thy person: hang him at a bough!
GAVESTON
My lord –   25
WARWICK
Soldiers, have him away.
But for thou wert the favourite of a king,

---

10 *broils* battles
14–16 ed. (Monster . . . strumpet / Traind . . . warres, / So . . . knights, Q)
15 *Greekish strumpet* Helen of Troy in Homer's *Iliad*, the great beauty, wife of
   Menelaus, King of Sparta, who fell in love with Paris, son of Priam, King of
   Troy; she ran away with Paris to Troy, and this was the pretext for the Trojan
   War. Though scornfully alluded to here, Helen is elsewhere celebrated in some
   of Marlowe's most famous lines (*Dr Faustus*, A-Text, 5.1.90–1).
   trained lured, baited
18 *buckler* shield, protect
20–2 ed. (Go . . . hence, / For . . . off: / *Gaueston* . . . turne: / It . . . cause, Q)
21 *warning* notice – in this case, of execution, giving the condemned man time to
   prepare himself spiritually. The insinuation that Gaveston needs little time
   suggests the irredeemable state of his soul.

Thou shalt have so much honour at our hands.

[*He gestures to indicate beheading*]

GAVESTON
I thank you all, my lords; then I perceive
That heading is one, and hanging is the other,   30
And death is all.

Enter [LORD MALTRAVERS,] EARL OF ARUNDEL

LANCASTER
How now, my lord of Arundel?
MALTRAVERS
My lords, King Edward greets you all by me.
WARWICK
Arundel, say your message.
MALTRAVERS   His majesty,
Hearing that you had taken Gaveston,   35
Entreateth you by me, that but he may
See him before he dies; for why, he says,
And sends you word, he knows that die he shall;
And if you gratify his grace so far,
He will be mindful of the courtesy.   40
WARWICK
How now?
GAVESTON   Renownèd Edward, how thy name
Revives poor Gaveston
WARWICK   No, it needeth not.
Arundel, we will gratify the King
In other matters; he must pardon us in this.
Soldiers, away with him.   45
GAVESTON
Why, my lord of Warwick,

28 *so much honour* Members of the nobility were, by privilege, exempt from hanging.
30 *heading* beheading
31 *death is all* i.e. death is still the same whether one is beheaded or hanged
   sd On the identification of Arundel with Maltravers, see the Note on the Text.
33 sp MALTRAVERS ed. (*Arun.* Q); also at ll. 34 (*Aru.*), 57, 65, 89
34–5 ed. (*one line in* Q)
36 *that* ed. (yet Q): the awkward Q reading probably arose from a compositorial
   misreading of copy 'y^t' (=that)
   but only. Edward is keeping his demands modest.
37 *for why* because
40 *be mindful* call to mind, take into consideration

Will not these delays beget my hopes?
I know it, lords, it is this life you aim at;
Yet grant King Edward this.

MORTIMER JUNIOR   Shalt thou appoint
What we shall grant? Soldiers, away with him!   50
[*To* MALTRAVERS] Thus we'll gratify the King:
We'll send his head by thee; let him bestow
His tears on that, for that is all he gets
Of Gaveston, or else his senseless trunk.

LANCASTER
Not so, my lord, lest he bestow more cost   55
In burying him than he hath ever earned.

MALTRAVERS
My lords, it is his majesty's request,
And in the honour of a king he swears
He will but talk with him and send him back.

WARWICK
When, can you tell? Arundel, no; we wot   60
He that the care of realm remits,
And drives his nobles to these exigents
For Gaveston, will, if he seize him once,
Violate any promise to possess him.

MALTRAVERS
Then if you will not trust his grace in keep,   65
My lords, I will be pledge for his return.

MORTIMER JUNIOR
It is honourable in thee to offer this,
But for we know thou art a noble gentleman,
We will not wrong thee so,
To make away a true man for a thief.   70

GAVESTON
How meanst thou, Mortimer? That is over-base.

---

47 *Will . . . hopes?* Gaveston is perturbed that the delay in his execution will not,
   after all, lead to a final meeting with Edward.
48 *aim at* intend (to take)
49–50 ed. (*Mor. iu.* Shalt . . . graunt? / Souldiers . . . him: Q)
60 *wot* know
61 *remits* surrenders, resigns
62 *exigents* exigencies, extreme measures
63 *seize* (zease Q; seaze Q3–4) take possession of
65 *in keep* with the loan (i.e. of Gaveston)
66 *pledge* security
70 *make away* murder (If Gaveston is not returned, Maltravers will be executed in
   his place.)

MORTIMER JUNIOR
Away, base groom, robber of kings' renown;
Question with thy companions and thy mates.
PEMBROKE
My lord Mortimer, and you my lords each one,
To gratify the King's request therein,   75
Touching the sending of this Gaveston,
Because his majesty so earnestly
Desires to see the man before his death,
I will upon mine honour undertake
To carry him and bring him back again,   80
Provided this, that you, my lord of Arundel
Will join with me.
WARWICK   Pembroke, what wilt thou do?
Cause yet more bloodshed? Is it not enough
That we have taken him, but must we now
Leave him on 'had I wist' and let him go?   85
PEMBROKE
My lords, I will not over-woo your honours,
But if you dare trust Pembroke with the prisoner,
Upon mine oath I will return him back.
MALTRAVERS
My lord of Lancaster, what say you in this?
LANCASTER
Why, I say, let him go on Pembroke's word.   90
PEMBROKE
And you, lord Mortimer?
MORTIMER JUNIOR
How say you, my lord of Warwick?
WARWICK
Nay, do your pleasures; I know how 'twill prove.
PEMBROKE
Then give him me.
GAVESTON   Sweet sovereign, yet I come
To see thee ere I die.
WARWICK [Aside]   Yet not perhaps,   95
If Warwick's wit and policy prevail.

73 *Question* argue
   companions often used as a term of contempt
85 *'had I wist'* had I known. Proverbial (Tilley H 8)
93 ed. (Nay . . . pleasures, / I . . . prooue. Q)
   do your pleasures i.e. do as you will
96 *wit* cunning
   policy contrivance, stratagem

MORTIMER JUNIOR
My lord of Pembroke, we deliver him you;
Return him on your honour. Sound away!

[*Trumpets sound.*] *Exeunt* [*all but*] PEMBROKE,
MALTRAVERS, GAVESTON *and* PEMBROKE'S MEN, *four
soldiers*[, *with* JAMES, *and* HORSE-BOY]

PEMBROKE
[*To* MALTRAVERS] My lord, you shall go with me;
My house is not far hence – out of the way   100
A little – but our men shall go along.
We that have pretty wenches to our wives,
Sir, must not come so near and balk their lips.
MALTRAVERS
'Tis very kindly spoke, my lord of Pembroke;
Your honour hath an adamant of power   105
To draw a prince.
PEMBROKE   So, my lord. Come hither, James.
I do commit this Gaveston to thee;
Be thou this night his keeper. In the morning
We will discharge thee of thy charge; be gone.
GAVESTON
Unhappy Gaveston, whither goest thou now?   110

Exit [GAVESTON, *with* PEMBROKE'S MEN *and* JAMES]

HORSE-BOY
My lord, we'll quickly be at Cobham.

Exeunt [PEMBROKE *and* MALTRAVERS, *with the* HORSE-
BOY *and soldiers*]

98 *Sound away!* He orders a trumpet call signalling a departure.
sd ed. (*Exeunt. / Manent Penbrooke, Mat. Gauest. & Pen- / brookes men, foure
souldiers.* Q)
103 *balk* neglect
104 *kindly* as befits *either* a nobleman *or* a husband
105 *adamant* magnet, lodestone
109 *discharge* relieve
charge responsibility
110 *Unhappy* unfortunate, unlucky
110 sd ed. (*Exit cum seruis Pen.* Q)
111 *Cobham* small town in Kent, near Gravesend
111 sd ed. (*Exeunt ambo.* Q)

[Scene 10]

Enter GAVESTON *mourning,* [*with* JAMES] *and the* EARL OF
PEMBROKE'S MEN

GAVESTON
O treacherous Warwick, thus to wrong thy friend!
JAMES
I see it is your life these arms pursue.
GAVESTON
Weaponless must I fall and die in bands.
O, must this day be period of my life,
Centre of all my bliss? An ye be men,   5
Speed to the King.

Enter WARWICK *and his company*

WARWICK   My lord of Pembroke's men,
Strive you no longer; I will have that Gaveston.
JAMES
Your lordship doth dishonour to yourself
And wrong our lord, your honourable friend.
WARWICK
No, James, it is my country's cause I follow.   10
Go, take the villain; soldiers, come away,
We'll make quick work. Commend me to your master,
My friend, and tell him that I watched it well.
[*To* GAVESTON] Come, let thy shadow parley with King
Edward.
GAVESTON
Treacherous Earl, shall I not see the King?   15
WARWICK
The king of heaven perhaps, no other king.
Away!
                    Exeunt WARWICK *and his men, with* GAVESTON. JAMES
                    remains with the others

1 *wrong thy friend* i.e. betray Pembroke
2 *arms* i.e. soldiers
3 *bands* bonds, fetters
4 *period* the end
5 *Centre* nadir, the greatest depth (possibly implying the centre of the earth)
6 *Speed* hasten, hurry
7 *Strive* struggle
13 *watched it well* i.e. guarded Gaveston efficiently
   booted not was useless
14 *shadow* ghost
17 sd ed. (*Exeunt Warwike and his men, with Gauest. / Manet Iames cum cæteris.* Q)

JAMES
　　Come fellows, it booted not for us to strive.
　　We will in haste go certify our lord.   *Exeunt*

[Scene 11]

Enter King EDWARD *and* SPENCER [JUNIOR, *and*
BALDOCK], *with drums and fifes*

EDWARD
　　I long to hear an answer from the barons
　　Touching my friend, my dearest Gaveston.
　　Ah, Spencer, not the riches of my realm
　　Can ransom him; ah, he is marked to die.
　　I know the malice of the younger Mortimer;   5
　　Warwick, I know, is rough, and Lancaster
　　Inexorable; and I shall never see
　　My lovely Piers, my Gaveston, again.
　　The barons overbear me with their pride.
SPENCER JUNIOR
　　Were I King Edward, England's sovereign,   10
　　Son to the lovely Eleanor of Spain,
　　Great Edward Longshanks' issue, would I bear
　　These braves, this rage, and suffer uncontrolled
　　These barons thus to beard me in my land,
　　In mine own realm? My lord, pardon my speech.   15
　　Did you retain your father's magnanimity,
　　Did you regard the honour of your name,
　　You would not suffer thus your majesty
　　Be counterbuffed of your nobility.
　　Strike off their heads, and let them preach on poles;   20
　　No doubt such lessons they will teach the rest,
　　As by their preachments they will profit much
　　And learn obedience to their lawful King.

18 *booted not* was useless

11 *Eleanor of Spain* Eleanor of Castile, first wife of Edward I
12 *Longshanks* the nickname ascribed to Edward I because of his long legs
13 *braves* defiant insults
　　suffer tolerate
14 *beard* defy with effrontery
16 *magnanimity* courage, fortitude
19 *counterbuffed of* opposed by
20 *preach on poles* See 1. 117 n.
22 *preachments* sermons

EDWARD
  Yea, gentle Spencer, we have been too mild,
  Too kind to them, but now have drawn our sword,   25
  And if they send me not my Gaveston,
  We'll steel it on their crest and poll their tops.
BALDOCK
  This haught resolve becomes your majesty,
  Not to be tied to their affection
  As though your highness were a schoolboy still,   30
  And must be awed and governed like a child.

> *Enter* HUGH SPENCER [SENIOR] *an old man, father to the young*
> SPENCER [JUNIOR], *with his truncheon, and soldiers*

SPENCER SENIOR
  Long live my sovereign, the noble Edward,
  In peace triumphant, fortunate in wars.
EDWARD
  Welcome, old man. Com'st thou in Edward's aid?
  Then tell thy prince of whence and what thou art.   35
SPENCER SENIOR
  Lo, with a band of bowmen and of pikes,
  Brown bills and targeteers, four hundred strong,
  Sworn to defend King Edward's royal right,
  I come in person to your majesty:
  Spencer, the father of Hugh Spencer there,   40
  Bound to your highness everlastingly
  For favours done in him unto us all.
EDWARD
  Thy father, Spencer?
SPENCER JUNIOR   True, an it like your grace,
  That pours in lieu of all your goodness shown,

---

27 *steel it* i.e. sharpen his sword
    poll their tops i.e. cut off their heads, punning on (i) the pollarding or cutting of
    tree-tops (ii) Spencer Junior's 'poles' (line 20 above)
28 *haught* haughty, lofty
29 *affection* desire, will
31 *awed* feared
31 sd 2 *truncheon* staff which symbolized authority
35 *of whence* from what place
    what thou art i.e. what is your name
36 *bowmen . . . pikes* Lances with sharp metal tips at both ends were driven into the
    ground just in front of the archers to protect them in battle.
37 *Brown bills* bronzed halberds (metonymic for the footsoldiers carrying them)
    targeteers shield-carrying infantrymen
43 *an it like* if it please

His life, my lord, before your princely feet.   45
EDWARD
Welcome ten thousand times, old man, again.
Spencer, this love, this kindness to thy King
Argues thy noble mind and disposition.
Spencer, I here create thee Earl of Wiltshire,
And daily will enrich thee with our favour   50
That, as the sunshine, shall reflect o'er thee.
Beside, the more to manifest our love,
Because we hear Lord Bruce doth sell his land
And that the Mortimers are in hand withal,
Thou shalt have crowns of us, t'outbid the barons;   55
And Spencer, spare them not, but lay it on.
Soldiers, a largess, and thrice welcome all.

Enter [ISABELLA] *the Queen and* [PRINCE EDWARD] *her son, and* LEVUNE, *a Frenchman*

SPENCER JUNIOR
My lord, here comes the Queen.
EDWARD   Madam, what news?
ISABELLA
News of dishonour, lord, and discontent:
Our friend Levune, faithful and full of trust,   60
Informeth us by letters and by words
That Lord Valois our brother, King of France,
Because your highness hath been slack in homage,
Hath seizèd Normandy into his hands.
These be the letters, this the messenger.   65
EDWARD
Welcome Levune. [*To* ISABELLA] Tush, Sib, if this be all,
Valois and I will soon be friends again.
But to my Gaveston – shall I never see,

---

47 For the first time, Edward addresses Spencer Senior by name; their relationship
    is now personal.
48 *Argues* proves. Ironically, this statement emphasizes the fact that Spencer Senior
    is not, by birth, a nobleman.
54 *in hand withal* i.e. engaged with this business
56 *spare them not* i.e. do not be frugal (with the money)
    lay it on be extravagant, flamboyant
57 *largess* liberal bestowal of money, bounty
57 sd ed.; after line 58a in Q
57 sd 2 ed. LEVUNE (*Lewne* Q; and throughout the text)
61 *words* oral report
66 *Sib* 'affectionate diminutive of Isabella' (Gill)

Never behold thee now? Madam, in this matter
We will employ you and your little son;   70
You shall go parley with the King of France.
Boy, see you bear you bravely to the King
And do your message with a majesty.

PRINCE EDWARD
Commit not to my youth things of more weight
Than fits a prince so young as I to bear.   75
And fear not, lord and father; heaven's great beams
On Atlas' shoulder shall not lie more safe
Than shall your charge committed to my trust.

ISABELLA
Ah, boy, this towardness makes thy mother fear
Thou art not marked to many days on earth.   80

EDWARD
Madam, we will that you with speed be shipped,
And this our son. Levune shall follow you
With all the haste we can dispatch him hence.
Choose of our lords to bear you company,
And go in peace; leave us in wars at home.   85

ISABELLA
Unnatural wars, where subjects brave their King:
God end them once. My lord, I take my leave
To make my preparation for France.

[*Exeunt* ISABELLA, PRINCE EDWARD *and* LEVUNE]

Enter LORD MALTRAVERS

EDWARD
What, Lord Maltravers, dost thou come alone?

MALTRAVERS
Yea, my good lord, for Gaveston is dead.   90

EDWARD
Ah, traitors, have they put my friend to death?
Tell me, Maltravers, died he ere thou cam'st,
Or didst thou see my friend to take his death?

MALTRAVERS
Neither, my lord, for as he was surprised,

---

77 *Atlas* In classical mythology, the Titan who carried the burden of the sky on his
   shoulders.
79 *towardness* boldness
80 Ironically, King Edward III reigned for fifty years (1327–77).
87 *once* i.e. once and for all
94 *surprised* ambushed

Begirt with weapons and with enemies round,   95
I did your highness' message to them all,
Demanding him of them – entreating rather –
And said, upon the honour of my name,
That I would undertake to carry him
Unto your highness, and to bring him back.   100
EDWARD
And tell me, would the rebels deny me that?
SPENCER JUNIOR
Proud recreants!
EDWARD   Yea, Spencer, traitors all.
MALTRAVERS
I found them at the first inexorable;
The Earl of Warwick would not bide the hearing,
Mortimer hardly; Pembroke and Lancaster   105
Spake least. And when they flatly had denied,
Refusing to receive me pledge for him,
The Earl of Pembroke mildly thus bespake:
'My lords, because our sovereign sends for him
And promiseth he shall be safe returned,   110
I will this undertake: to have him hence
And see him re-delivered to your hands.'
EDWARD
Well, and how fortunes that he came not?
SPENCER JUNIOR
Some treason or some villainy was cause.
MALTRAVERS
The Earl of Warwick seized him on his way,   115
For, being delivered unto Pembroke's men,
Their lord rode home, thinking his prisoner safe;
But ere he came, Warwick in ambush lay,
And bare him to his death, and in a trench
Struck off his head, and marched unto the camp.   120
SPENCER JUNIOR
A bloody part, flatly against law of arms.
EDWARD
O, shall I speak, or shall I sigh and die?

---

95 *Begirt* encompassed, enclosed
   round i.e. encircling, surrounding
102 *recreants* breakers of allegiance
104 *bide* endure, abide
113 *fortunes* chances
121 *part* action, deed
   flatly absolutely

SPENCER JUNIOR
My lord, refer your vengeance to the sword
Upon these barons; hearten up your men.
Let them not unrevenged murder your friends.   125
Advance your standard, Edward, in the field,
And march to fire them from their starting holes.
EDWARD
[*Kneeling*] By earth, the common mother of us all,
By heaven and all the moving orbs thereof,
By this right hand and by my father's sword,   130
And all the honours 'longing to my crown,
I will have heads and lives for him as many
As I have manors, castles, towns, and towers.
Treacherous Warwick! Traitorous Mortimer!
If I be England's king, in lakes of gore   135
Your headless trunks, your bodies will I trail,
That you may drink your fill and quaff in blood,
And stain my royal standard with the same,
That so my bloody colours may suggest
Remembrance of revenge immortally   140
On your accursèd traitorous progeny –
You villains that have slain my Gaveston.
And in this place of honour and of trust,
Spencer, sweet Spencer, I adopt thee here;
And merely of our love we do create thee   145
Earl of Gloucester and Lord Chamberlain,
Despite of times, despite of enemies.
SPENCER JUNIOR
My lord, here is a messenger from the barons

---

123 *refer* assign
126 *Advance your standard* raise your ensign
     in the field in battle
127 *fire* smoke out
     starting holes place of refuge for animals
128 sd ed. (*Edward kneeles, and saith.* Q)
129 *moving orbs* in Ptolemaic cosmology, the moving concentric spheres surrounding
     the Earth; alternatively, the sun, moon, and planets, all of which were thought
     to orbit the Earth
130 *father's sword* The sword was wielded by monarchs as a symbol of divine justice
     on Earth; cf. Romans 13:1–4.
131 *'longing* belonging
141 *progeny* lineage
145 *merely . . . love* i.e. rather than by right of succession; Spencer Junior was only a
     retainer of the previous Earl of Gloucester
148 *here is* ed. (heres is Q1–2; heers Q3; heer's Q4)

Desires access unto your majesty.
EDWARD
Admit him near.   150

Enter the HERALD *from the Barons, with his coat of arms*

HERALD
Long live King Edward, England's lawful lord.
EDWARD
So wish not they, iwis, that sent thee hither.
Thou com'st from Mortimer and his complices –
A ranker rout of rebels never was.
Well, say thy message.   155
HERALD
The barons up in arms, by me salute
Your highness with long life and happiness,
And bid me say as plainer to your grace,
That if without effusion of blood
You will this grief have ease and remedy,   160
That from your princely person you remove
This Spencer, as a putrefying branch
That deads the royal vine whose golden leaves
Impale your princely head, your diadem,
Whose brightness such pernicious upstarts dim,   165
Say they; and lovingly advise your grace
To cherish virtue and nobility,
And have old servitors in high esteem,
And shake off smooth dissembling flatterers.
This granted, they, their honours, and their lives   170
Are to your highness vowed and consecrate.

151, 156 sp ed. HERALD (Q *Messen.*)
152 *iwis* assuredly
153 *complices* confederates, conspirators
154 *rout* (route Q; roote Q2–3; rout Q4); unruly crowd
158 *plainer* complainant, one who brings an accusation
159 *effusion* shedding (four syllables)
163 *deads* deadens
       royal vine Edward's crown was, in fact, decorated with four large and four small
       strawberry leaves. See *Boutell's Heraldry* (revised by J. P. Brooke-Little, London,
       1970, p. 184).
164 *Impale* encircle
       diadem crown
168 *old servitors* retainers of long standing (Forker)
169 *smooth* (i) plausible (ii) obsequious
171 *consecrate* made sacred

SPENCER JUNIOR
   Ah, traitors, will they still display their pride?
EDWARD
   Away! Tarry no answer, but be gone.
   Rebels! Will they appoint their sovereign
   His sports, his pleasures, and his company?   175
   Yet ere thou go, see how I do divorce
   Spencer from me.   *Embrace[s* SPENCER JUNIOR]
                  Now get thee to thy lords,
   And tell them I will come to chastise them
   For murdering Gaveston. Hie thee, get thee gone;
   Edward with fire and sword follows at thy heels.   180

                              [*Exit* HERALD]

   My lords, perceive you how these rebels swell?
   Soldiers, good hearts, defend your sovereign's right,
   For now, even now, we march to make them stoop.
   Away!   *Exeunt*

                        [Scene 12]

          Alarums, excursions, a great fight, and a retreat

          Enter [EDWARD] *the King,* SPENCER [SENIOR], SPENCER
             JUNIOR, *and the noblemen of the King's side*

EDWARD
   Why do we sound retreat? Upon them, lords!
   This day I shall pour vengeance with my sword
   On those proud rebels that are up in arms,
   And do confront and countermand their King.

173 *Tarry* wait for
174 *appoint* order, grant
175 *sports* pastimes
177 sd ed. (after 'deuorce' and 'lords,' respectively Q *Embrace / Spencer.*)
179 *Hie* hasten, hurry
181 *lords* ed. (lord Q)
       swell grow proud
183 *make them stoop* i.e. humiliate them

  0 sd 1 *Alarums* battle-cries, trumpet signals
       excursions rush of soldiers across the stage
  4 *countermand* oppose

SPENCER JUNIOR
   I doubt it not, my lord; right will prevail.　　　　5
SPENCER SENIOR
   'Tis not amiss, my liege, for either part
   To breathe a while; our men with sweat and dust
   All choked well near, begin to faint for heat,
   And this retire refresheth horse and man.

Enter the Barons, MORTIMER [JUNIOR], LANCASTER,
[KENT,] WARWICK, PEMBROKE, *with the others*

SPENCER JUNIOR
   Here come the rebels.　　　　　　　　　　10
MORTIMER JUNIOR
   Look, Lancaster,
   Yonder is Edward among his flatterers.
LANCASTER
   And there let him be,
   Till he pay dearly for their company.
WARWICK
   And shall, or Warwick's sword shall smite in vain.　　15
EDWARD
   What, rebels, do you shrink and sound retreat?
MORTIMER JUNIOR
   No, Edward, no; thy flatterers faint and fly.
LANCASTER
   Thou'd best betimes forsake thee and their trains,
   For they'll betray thee, traitors as they are.
SPENCER JUNIOR
   Traitor on thy face, rebellious Lancaster.　　　20
PEMBROKE
   Away, base upstart; brav'st thou nobles thus?
SPENCER SENIOR
   A noble attempt and honourable deed
   Is it not, trow ye, to assemble aid
   And levy arms against your lawful King?

   9 *retire* (i) respite (ii) retreat
   9 sd ed.; after line 10 in Q
  11–12 ed. (Looke . . . his / flatterers. Q)
  13–14 ed. (And . . . for / their companie. Q)
  18 *Thou'd* ed. (Th'ad Q) thou had
    betimes in good time
    trains tricks, political stratagems
  23 *trow* know, think

EDWARD
    For which ere long their heads shall satisfy   25
    T'appease the wrath of their offended King.
MORTIMER JUNIOR
    Then, Edward, thou wilt fight it to the last,
    And rather bathe thy sword in subjects' blood
    Than banish that pernicious company?
EDWARD
    Ay, traitors all! Rather than thus be braved,   30
    Make England's civil towns huge heaps of stones
    And ploughs to go about our palace gates.
WARWICK
    A desperate and unnatural resolution.
    Alarum to the fight!
    Saint George for England and the barons' right!   35
EDWARD
    Saint George for England and King Edward's right!

        [*Exeunt* WARWICK *with his men at one door and* EDWARD *with
                                    his men at the other*]

                        [Scene 13]

        [*Alarums.*] *Enter* EDWARD, [SPENCER SENIOR, SPENCER
        JUNIOR, BALDOCK, LEVUNE, *and soldiers*] *with the Barons*
            [KENT, WARWICK, LANCASTER, *and* MORTIMER JUNIOR
                        and others] *captives*

EDWARD
    Now, lusty lords, now not by chance of war
    But justice of the quarrel and the cause,
    Vailed is your pride. Methinks you hang the heads,
    But we'll advance them, traitors! Now 'tis time
    To be avenged on you for all your braves   5
    And for the murder of my dearest friend,

25 *satisfy* atone, make amends
34–5 ed. (Alarum . . . England, / And . . . right. Q)
35 *Saint George* Patron Saint of England (not adopted until Edward III's reign)

0 sd 3 *and others* i.e. 'the rest' who are ordered to be executed at ll. 33–4
3 *Vailed* lowered
4 *advance* i.e. raise their severed heads on pikes
5 *braves* see 11. 13 n.

To whom right well you knew our soul was knit:
Good Piers of Gaveston, my sweet favourite –
Ah rebels, recreants, you made him away!

KENT

Brother, in regard of thee and of thy land,   10
Did they remove that flatterer from thy throne.

EDWARD

So, sir, you have spoke; away, avoid our presence.

[*Exit* KENT]

Accursèd wretches, was't in regard of us,
When we had sent our messenger to request
He might be spared to come to speak with us,   15
And Pembroke undertook for his return,
That thou, proud Warwick, watched the prisoner,
Poor Piers, and headed him against law of arms?
For which thy head shall overlook the rest
As much as thou in rage outwent'st the rest.   20

WARWICK

Tyrant, I scorn thy threats and menaces;
'Tis but temporal that thou canst inflict.

LANCASTER

The worst is death, and better die to live,
Than live in infamy under such a king.

EDWARD

Away with them, my lord of Winchester,   25
These lusty leaders, Warwick and Lancaster.
I charge you roundly off with both their heads.
Away!

WARWICK

Farewell, vain world.

10 *in regard* out of consideration
12 *avoid* depart from
17 *watched* kept watch over
18 *headed* beheaded
19 *head . . . the rest* i.e. his severed head will be mounted higher than the others'
22 *but temporal* Edward can only inflict physical, not spiritual, suffering.
23 *The worst is death* Cf. *Richard II*, 'The worst is death, and death will have his day' (3.2.99).
23–4 *better . . . infamy* proverbial (Tilley H 576)
25 *Winchester* Spencer Senior was created Earl of Wiltshire at 11. 49, but is here addressed as Marquess of Winchester. In Marlowe's time, the two titles were held by the same person, William Paulet (c. 1532–98).
27 *roundly* without hesitation
27–8 ed. (*one line in* Q)
29 *vain* worthless, futile

LANCASTER   Sweet Mortimer, farewell.

[*Exeunt* WARWICK *and* LANCASTER, *guarded by*
SPENCER SENIOR]

MORTIMER JUNIOR
England, unkind to thy nobility,   30
Groan for this grief; behold how thou art maimed.
EDWARD
Go take that haughty Mortimer to the Tower;
There see him safe bestowed. And for the rest,
Do speedy execution on them all.
Begone!   35
MORTIMER JUNIOR
What, Mortimer! Can ragged stony walls
Immure thy virtue that aspires to heaven?
No, Edward, England's scourge, it may not be;
Mortimer's hope surmounts his fortune far.

[*Exit* MORTIMER JUNIOR *guarded*]

EDWARD
Sound drums and trumpets! March with me my friends; 40
Edward this day hath crowned him King anew.

Exit[, *attended*]. SPENCER [JUNIOR],
LEVUNE *and* BALDOCK *remain*

SPENCER JUNIOR
Levune, the trust that we repose in thee
Begets the quiet of King Edward's land.
Therefore be gone in haste, and with advice
Bestow that treasure on the lords of France;   45
That therewithal enchanted, like the guard
That suffered Jove to pass in showers of gold
To Danaë, all aid may be denied

34–5 ed. (*one line in* Q)
36 *ragged* rugged
37 *Immure* enclose (within walls)
    virtue power
38 *scourge* often used by Marlowe to describe a ruler who lays waste a nation. Cf.
    2 Tamburlaine, 'Be all a scourge and terror to the world' (1.3.63)
39 *surmounts* surpasses, rises above
41 sd ed. (*Manent Spencer filius, Lewne & Baldock.* Q)
42 *repose* place
43 *Begets* will produce, obtain
46 *therewithal* ed. (therewith all Q)
46–8 *like . . . Danaë* See 6. 53 n.

To Isabel the Queen, that now in France
Makes friends, to cross the seas with her young son,   50
And step into his father's regiment.
LEVUNE
That's it these barons and the subtle Queen
Long levelled at.
BALDOCK   Yea, but Levune, thou seest
These barons lay their heads on blocks together;
What they intend, the hangman frustrates clean.   55
LEVUNE
Have you no doubts, my lords; I'll clap 's close
Among the lords of France with England's gold
That Isabel shall make her plaints in vain,
And France shall be obdurate with her tears.
SPENCER JUNIOR
Then make for France amain; Levune, away!   60
Proclaim King Edward's wars and victories.   *Exeunt*

[Scene 14]

Enter EDMUND [THE EARL OF KENT]

KENT
Fair blows the wind for France; blow, gentle gale,
Till Edmund be arrived for England's good.
Nature, yield to my country's cause in this:
A brother – no, a butcher of thy friends –
Proud Edward, dost thou banish me thy presence?   5
But I'll to France, and cheer the wrongèd Queen,
And certify what Edward's looseness is.
Unnatural King, to slaughter noblemen
And cherish flatterers. Mortimer, I stay

51 *regiment* rule, authority
52 *subtle* cunning, insidious
53 *levelled at* ed. (leuied at Q) aimed at
55 *clean* completely, absolutely
56 *clap 's* ed. (claps Q); 'clap us'; strike a bargain; clap usually referred to the clapping of hands when securing a transaction
    close secretly
59 *obdurate* unyielding
60 *amain* at once

1 *gentle* not stormy, but also implying courtesy or generosity
7 *looseness* (i) carelessness, incompetence (ii) sexual misconduct
9 *stay* await

Thy sweet escape; stand gracious, gloomy night   10
To his device.

Enter MORTIMER [JUNIOR] *disguised*

MORTIMER JUNIOR
Holla! Who walketh there? Is't you my lord?
KENT
Mortimer, 'tis I;
But hath thy potion wrought so happily?
MORTIMER JUNIOR
It hath, my lord; the warders all asleep,   15
I thank them, gave me leave to pass in peace.
But hath your grace got shipping unto France?
KENT
Fear it not.   *Exeunt*

[Scene 15]

Enter [ISABELLA] *the Queen and her son* [PRINCE
EDWARD]

ISABELLA
Ah boy, our friends do fail us all in France;
The lords are cruel and the King unkind.
What shall we do?
PRINCE EDWARD   Madam, return to England
And please my father well, and then a fig
For all my uncle's friendship here in France.   5
I warrant you, I'll win his highness quickly;
A loves me better than a thousand Spencers.
ISABELLA
Ah boy, thou art deceived at least in this,
To think that we can yet be tuned together.

10–11 Kent invokes the darkness of night to aid Mortimer Junior's escape.

11 *device* stratagem, intent

13–14 ed. (*Mortimer . . . so* / happilie? Q)

14 *thy potion . . . happily?* i.e. have the guards been successfully drugged?

16 *gave me leave* allowed me

4 *a fig* obscene expression of contempt; usually accompanied by a phallic gesture
in which the thumb was thrust into the mouth or between two closed fingers.
Proverbial (Tilley F 210)

6 *warrant* assure

7 *A* unstressed form of 'he'

9 *yet* still

No, no, we jar too far. Unkind Valois!   10
Unhappy Isabel! When France rejects,
Whither, O whither dost thou bend thy steps?

Enter SIR JOHN OF HAINAULT

SIR JOHN
Madam, what cheer?
ISABELLA   Ah, good Sir John of Hainault,
Never so cheerless, nor so far distressed.
SIR JOHN
I hear, sweet lady, of the King's unkindness.   15
But droop not, madam; noble minds contemn
Despair. Will your grace with me to Hainault
And there stay time's advantage with your son?
How say you, my lord, will you go with your friends,
And shake off all our fortunes equally?   20
PRINCE EDWARD
So pleaseth the Queen, my mother, me it likes.
The King of England nor the court of France
Shall have me from my gracious mother's side,
Till I be strong enough to break a staff,
And then have at the proudest Spencer's head.   25
SIR JOHN
Well said, my lord.
ISABELLA
Oh, my sweet heart, how do I moan thy wrongs,
Yet triumph in the hope of thee, my joy.
Ah, sweet Sir John, even to the utmost verge
Of Europe, or the shore of Tanaïs,   30

---

10 *jar* (i) become discordant, playing upon the metaphor of the previous line (ii)
    quarrel
11 *Unhappy* unfortunate, unlucky
12 *bend . . . steps* i.e. what course of action should I next take?
13 *what cheer* i.e. what is your mood, disposition?
16 *contemn* despise, disregard
17 *Hainault* Flemish county in the Low Countries, bordering France
20 *shake off* cast off
21 *So* as it
24 *staff* a lance or quarter-staff, used (and broken) in combat
25 *have at* attack, strike at (imperative)
27 *moan* lament (aloud)
29 *utmost verge* i.e. the furthest limit
30 *Tanaïs* the Latin name for the River Don which the Elizabethans regarded as the
    boundary between Europe and Asia

Will we with thee to Hainault, so we will.
The Marquis is a noble gentleman;
His grace, I dare presume, will welcome me.

Enter EDMUND [THE EARL OF KENT] *and* MORTIMER
[JUNIOR]

But who are these?
KENT   Madam, long may you live
Much happier than your friends in England do.   35
ISABELLA
Lord Edmund and Lord Mortimer alive!
Welcome to France. The news was here, my lord,
That you were dead, or very near your death.
MORTIMER JUNIOR
Lady, the last was truest of the twain;
But Mortimer, reserved for better hap,   40
Hath shaken off the thraldom of the Tower,
[*To* PRINCE EDWARD] And lives t'advance your standard,
    good my lord.
PRINCE EDWARD
How mean you, an the King my father lives?
No, my lord Mortimer, not I, I trow.
ISABELLA
Not, son? Why not? I would it were no worse;   45
But gentle lords, friendless we are in France.
MORTIMER JUNIOR
Monsieur le Grand, a noble friend of yours,
Told us at our arrival all the news:
How hard the nobles, how unkind the King
Hath shewed himself. But madam, right makes room   50
Where weapons want; and though a many friends
Are made away – as Warwick, Lancaster,

---

32 *Marquis* i.e. Sir John's brother, William, Count of Hainault
33 sd ed.; after line 34a in Q
40 *hap* fortune
41 *thraldom* servitude, bondage
42 *t'advance your standard* i.e. raise the banner or ensign of battle
44 *trow* think, reckon
47 *Monsieur le Grand* an invented character with no historical original
49 *hard* difficult, obdurate
    unkind unnatural (to his sister, Isabella)
    the King i.e. the King of France
50 *makes room* makes way
51 *want* i.e. are required   *a many* many
52 *made away* i.e. dead (implicitly by murder and treachery)

And others of our party and faction –
Yet have we friends, assure your grace, in England
Would cast up caps and clap their hands for joy,   55
To see us there appointed for our foes.

KENT
Would all were well and Edward well reclaimed,
For England's honour, peace, and quietness.

MORTIMER JUNIOR
But by the sword, my lord, it must be deserved.
The King will ne'er forsake his flatterers.   60

SIR JOHN
My lords of England, sith the ungentle King
Of France refuseth to give aid of arms
To this distressèd queen his sister here,
Go you with her to Hainault. Doubt ye not,
We will find comfort, money, men, and friends   65
Ere long, to bid the English King a base.
How say, young prince, what think you of the match?

PRINCE EDWARD
I think King Edward will outrun us all.

ISABELLA
Nay son, not so; and you must not discourage
Your friends that are so forward in your aid.   70

KENT
Sir John of Hainault, pardon us, I pray;
These comforts that you give our woeful Queen
Bind us in kindness all at your command.

ISABELLA
Yea, gentle brother; and the God of heaven
Prosper your happy motion, good Sir John.   75

MORTIMER JUNIOR
This noble gentleman, forward in arms,
Was born, I see, to be our anchor-hold.

---

55 *cast up caps* i.e. throw caps into the air as a sign of joy
56 *appointed* armed, prepared for battle
57 *reclaimed* subdued
59 *deserved* earned
61 *sith* since
66 *bid . . . a base* challenge to risk capture (from 'prisoner's base', a children's game
    involving running between two 'bases', between which the players might be
    caught by their opponents)
67 *match* game
74 *brother* i.e. brother-in-law
75 *motion* proposal
76 *forward* ardent

Sir John of Hainault, be it thy renown
That England's Queen and nobles in distress
Have been by thee restored and comforted.   80
SIR JOHN
Madam, along, and you, my lord, with me,
That England's peers may Hainault's welcome see.

[*Exeunt*]

[Scene 16]

Enter [EDWARD] *the King,* MALTRAVERS, *the two*
SPENCERS, [SENIOR *and* JUNIOR,] *with others*

EDWARD
Thus after many threats of wrathful war,
Triumpheth England's Edward with his friends;
And triumph Edward with his friends uncontrolled.
[*To* SPENCER JUNIOR] My lord of Gloucester, do you hear
the news?
SPENCER JUNIOR
What news, my lord?   5
EDWARD
Why man, they say there is great execution
Done through the realm. My lord of Arundel,
You have the note, have you not?
MALTRAVERS
From the Lieutenant of the Tower, my lord.
EDWARD
I pray let us see it. What have we there?   10
Read it Spencer.

SPENCER [JUNIOR] *reads their names*†

Why so, they 'barked apace a month ago;
Now, on my life, they'll neither bark nor bite.

---

3 *uncontrolled* without censure
8 *note* official list
11 sd SPENCER [JUNIOR] *reads . . . names* The details of those who have been executed are not included in the control text, thus creating some staging difficulties.
   Holinshed supplies the list reproduced in the ruled box on p. 85; if required, this
   might be interpolated in performance.
12 *'barked* embarked on committing treason (Forker)
   apace swiftly
13 *neither bark nor bite* Edward puns on the previous line, introducing a proverbial
   meaning (Tilley B 85, B 86).

Now, sirs, the news from France; Gloucester, I trow
The lords of France love England's gold so well   15
As Isabella gets no aid from thence.
What now remains? Have you proclaimed, my lord,
Reward for them can bring in Mortimer?

SPENCER JUNIOR
My lord, we have; and if he be in England,
A will be had ere long, I doubt it not.   20

EDWARD
If, dost thou say? Spencer, as true as death,
He is in England's ground; our port masters
Are not so careless of their King's command.

Enter a POST [*with letters*]

How now, what news with thee? From whence come these?

POST
Letters, my lord, and tidings forth of France   25
To you, my lord of Gloucester, from Levune.

EDWARD
Read.

SPENCER JUNIOR (*Reads the letter*)
'My duty to your honour premised, *etcetera*, I have according to instructions in that behalf, dealt with the King
of France's lords, and effected, that the Queen, all discon-   30
tented and discomforted, is gone. Whither? If you ask,
with Sir John of Hainault, brother to the Marquis, into
Flanders. With them are gone Lord Edmund and the Lord
Mortimer, having in their company divers of your nation,

.

15 *love England's gold* i.e. Edward's bribe has worked
16 *Isabella* ed. (*Isabell* Q)
20 *A* he, i.e. Mortimer Junior
  had captured (Forker)
21 *as true as death* proverbial (Tilley D 136)
27–8 ed. (Reade. / *Spencer reades the letter.* Q)
28 *premised* ed. (promised Q; premised Q2); that which serves as a formal prefix or
  introduction to a report
  etcetera ed. (&c. Q)
28–9 *according . . . in that behalf* i.e. with respect to Edward's instructions
30 *France's* ed. (Fraunce his Q)
  effected i.e. have caused, brought about
31 *discomforted* discouraged

†Extract from Holinshed, *Chronicles of England,*
Scotland, and Ireland (1587 ed., vol. 3, p. 331)

... the Lord William Tuchet, the Lord William Fitzwilliam,
the Lord Warren de Lisle, the Lord Henry Bradborne, and the
Lord William Chenie, barons, with John Page, an esquire,
were drawn and hanged at Pomfret... and then shortly after,
Roger Lord Clifford, John Lord Mowbray, and Sir Gosein   5
D'Eivill, barons, were drawn and hanged at York. At Bristol in
like manner were executed Sir Henry de Willington and Sir
Henry Montfort, baronets; and at Gloucester, the Lord John
Gifford and Sir William Elmebridge, knight; and at London,
the Lord Henry Tyes, baron; at Winchelsea, Sir Thomas   10
Culpepper, knight; at Windsor, the Lord Francis de Aldham,
baron; and at Canterbury, the Lord Bartholomew de
Badlesmere and the Lord Bartholomew de Ashburnham,
barons. Also, at Cardiff in Wales, Sir William Fleming, knight,
was executed. Divers were executed in their counties, as Sir   15
Thomas Mandit and others.

4 *Pomfret* Pontefract
15 *counties* ed. (*Holinshed reads* countries)

and others; and, as constant report goeth, they intend to   35
give King Edward battle in England sooner than he can
look for them. This is all the news of import.
                    Your honour's in all service, Levune.'
EDWARD
Ah, villains, hath that Mortimer escaped?
With him is Edmund gone associate?   40
And will Sir John of Hainault lead the round?
Welcome, i' God's name, madam, and your son;
England shall welcome you and all your rout.
Gallop apace bright Phoebus through the sky,
And dusky night, in rusty iron car,   45
Between you both shorten the time, I pray,

35 *constant* consistent, reliable
35–7 *they intend . . . for them* i.e. they will take the initiative in challenging Edward
   to fight before he is ready
37 *import* importance
41 *round* dance
43 *rout* unruly followers
44 *Phoebus* Phoebus Apollo, the sun god of classical mythology, who drove the sun
   across the sky in a chariot
45 *dusky night . . . car* Cf. *1 Tamburlaine*, 'ugly Darkness with her rusty coach'
   (5.1.294).

That I may see that most desirèd day
When we may meet these traitors in the field.
Ah, nothing grieves me but my little boy,
Is thus misled to countenance their ills.   50
Come, friends, to Bristol, there to make us strong;
And, winds, as equal be to bring them in
As you injurious were to bear them forth.   [*Exeunt*]

[Scene 17]

Enter [ISABELLA] *the Queen, her son* [PRINCE EDWARD],
EDMUND [THE EARL OF KENT], MORTIMER [JUNIOR], *and*
SIR JOHN [OF HAINAULT, *with soldiers*]

ISABELLA
Now lords, our loving friends and countrymen,
Welcome to England all. With prosperous winds
Our kindest friends in Belgia have we left,
To cope with friends at home. A heavy case,
When force to force is knit, and sword and glaive   5
In civil broils makes kin and countrymen
Slaughter themselves in others, and their sides
With their own weapons gored. But what's the help?
Misgoverned kings are cause of all this wrack;
And Edward, thou art one among them all,   10
Whose looseness hath betrayed thy land to spoil
And made the channels overflow with blood.
Of thine own people patron shouldst thou be,

---

50 *countenance* favour, support
   ills sins, wickedness
51 *strong* resolute, determined
52 *equal* just

2 *prosperous* favourable
3 *Belgia* the Low Countries
4 *cope* engage in battle
   friends kinsfolk, relatives
   heavy case sad predicament
5 *glaive* variously used of the spear, halberd, and broadsword
6 *civil broils* i.e. civil wars
8 *help* remedy
9 *Misgoverned* unruly
   wrack destruction
11 *looseness* (i) frivolous, careless behaviour (ii) lasciviousness
13–14a ed. (*one line in* Q)
13 *patron* father-figure (and hence an example)

But thou –
MORTIMER JUNIOR
        Nay madam, if you be a warrior,
Ye must not grow so passionate in speeches.   15
Lords, sith that we are by sufferance of heaven
Arrived and armèd in this prince's right,
Here for our country's cause swear we to him
All homage, fealty, and forwardness.
And for the open wrongs and injuries   20
Edward hath done to us, his Queen, and land,
We come in arms to wreak it with the sword,
That England's Queen in peace may repossess
Her dignities and honours, and withal
We may remove these flatterers from the King,   25
That havocs England's wealth and treasury.
SIR JOHN
Sound trumpets, my lord, and forward let us march;
Edward will think we come to flatter him.
KENT
I would he never had been flattered more.

                    [Sound trumpets. Exeunt]

                    [Scene 18]

        Enter [EDWARD] the King, BALDOCK, and SPENCER
              [JUNIOR], flying about the stage

SPENCER JUNIOR
    Fly, fly, my lord! The Queen is over-strong;
    Her friends do multiply and yours do fail.
    Shape we our course to Ireland, there to breathe.
EDWARD
    What, was I born to fly and run away,

16 *sufferance* permission
19 *fealty* loyalty, fidelity
   forwardness eagerness
22 *wreak* ed. (wrecke Q: a variant form of wreak) avenge
   sword ed. (swords Q; sworde Q2–3; sword Q4)
26 *havocs . . . treasury* i.e. misuses (literally lays waste) public money by indiscrim-
   inate spending

1 *Fly* run
2 *multiply* increase
  fail (i) become exhausted (ii) fall, die (iii) decline in number
3 *Shape* steer

And leave the Mortimers conquerors behind?   5
Give me my horse, and let's r'enforce our troops,
And in this bed of honour die with fame.

BALDOCK
O no, my lord; this princely resolution
Fits not the time. Away! We are pursued.   [*Exeunt*]

[*Enter*] EDMUND [THE EARL OF KENT] *alone with a sword
and target*

KENT
This way he fled, but I am come too late.   10
Edward, alas, my heart relents for thee.
Proud traitor Mortimer, why dost thou chase
Thy lawful King, thy sovereign, with thy sword?
Vile wretch, and why hast thou of all unkind,
Borne arms against thy brother and thy King?   15
Rain showers of vengeance on my cursèd head,
Thou God, to whom in justice it belongs
To punish this unnatural revolt.
Edward, this Mortimer aims at thy life;
O fly him then! But Edmund, calm this rage;   20
Dissemble or thou diest, for Mortimer
And Isabel do kiss while they conspire;
And yet she bears a face of love, forsooth.
Fie on that love that hatcheth death and hate!
Edmund, away; Bristol to Longshanks' blood   25
Is false. Be not found single for suspect;
Proud Mortimer pries near into thy walks.

Enter [ISABELLA] *the Queen*, MORTIMER [JUNIOR], *the
young* PRINCE [EDWARD], *and* SIR JOHN OF HAINAULT

---

5 *the Mortimers* Gill notes that the historical Mortimer Senior was, at this point,
   already dead.
6 *r'enforce* urge, encourage (once more)
7 *bed of honour* i.e. England
9 sd 3 *target* lightweight shield
14 *Vile wretch* Kent addresses himself
   unkind unnatural (because he has acted against his own brother)
19 *aims . . . life* i.e. intends to kill Edward
21 *Dissemble* i.e. be a hypocrite, be deceptive
23 *forsooth* certainly, in truth (said with irony and contempt)
25–6 *Bristol . . . false* i.e. the Mayor of Bristol has betrayed the son of King Edward
   I (cf. 11. 12 n.)
26 *single* alone, by oneself
   for suspect i.e. for this causes suspicion
27 *walks* movements

ISABELLA
  Successful battles gives the God of kings
  To them that fight in right and fear his wrath.
  Since then successfully we have prevailed,   30
  Thanks be heaven's great architect and you.
  Ere farther we proceed, my noble lords,
  We here create our well-belovèd son,
  Of love and care unto his royal person,
  Lord Warden of the realm; and sith the fates   35
  Have made his father so infortunate,
  Deal you, my lords, in this, my loving lords,
  As to your wisdoms fittest seems in all.
KENT
  Madam, without offence, if I may ask,
  How will you deal with Edward in his fall?   40
PRINCE EDWARD
  Tell me, good uncle, what Edward do you mean?
KENT
  Nephew, your father; I dare not call him King.
MORTIMER JUNIOR
  My lord of Kent, what needs these questions?
  'Tis not in her controlment, nor in ours,
  But as the realm and Parliament shall please,   45
  So shall your brother be disposèd of.
  [*Aside to* ISABELLA] I like not this relenting mood in
    Edmund;
  Madam, 'tis good to look to him betimes.
ISABELLA [*Aside to* MORTIMER JUNIOR]
  My lord, the Mayor of Bristol knows our mind?
MORTIMER JUNIOR
  [*Aside*] Yea, madam, and they 'scape not easily   50

---

31 *you* i.e. Isabella's allies
34 *Of* Out of
35 *Lord Warden* viceroy, usually appointed during a king's minority or absence
    fates goddesses of destiny
36 *infortunate* unfortunate
37 *Deal* act, proceed
38 *fittest* most suitable, agreeable
41 'Kent is ungently reproved for lack of respect (by not referring to Edward by his
    title)' (Gill).
44 *controlment* (i) power (ii) ability to restrain
47 *relenting* pitying
48 *look to him* i.e. in anticipation of a change of loyalties
    betimes in good time
49 *knows our mind* i.e. is acquainted with our intentions

That fled the field.

ISABELLA   Baldock is with the King;
A goodly chancellor, is he not, my lord?

SIR JOHN
So are the Spencers, the father and the son.

KENT
[*To himself*] This Edward is the ruin of the realm.

Enter RHYS AP HOWELL, *and the* MAYOR OF BRISTOL, *with*
SPENCER [SENIOR, *guarded by soldiers*]

RHYS AP HOWELL
God save Queen Isabel and her princely son.   55
Madam, the Mayor and citizens of Bristol,
In sign of love and duty to this presence,
Present by me this traitor to the state –
Spencer, the father to that wanton Spencer,
That, like the lawless Catiline of Rome,   60
Revelled in England's wealth and treasury.

ISABELLA
We thank you all.

MORTIMER JUNIOR   Your loving care in this
Deserveth princely favours and rewards.
But where's the King and the other Spencer fled?

RHYS AP HOWELL
Spencer the son, created Earl of Gloucester,   65
Is with that smooth-tongued scholar Baldock gone,
And shipped but late for Ireland with the King.

MORTIMER JUNIOR
Some whirlwind fetch them back, or sink them all!
They shall be started thence, I doubt it not.

PRINCE EDWARD
Shall I not see the King my father yet?   70

KENT
[*Aside*] Unhappy Edward, chased from England's bounds.

SIR JOHN
Madam, what resteth? Why stand ye in a muse?

57 *presence* i.e. royal presence
60 *Catiline* Lucius Sergius Catalina (d. 62 B.C.), a corrupt Roman nobleman who
    was a byword for treason in the 1590s
67 *but late* just lately
69 *started* forced out (as an animal driven from its hiding-place)
71 *Unhappy* ed. (Vnhappies Q)
    bounds territory
72 *resteth* remains to be done
    in a muse in thought, perplexed

ISABELLA
I rue my lord's ill fortune, but, alas,
Care of my country called me to this war.
MORTIMER JUNIOR
Madam, have done with care and sad complaint;   75
Your King hath wronged your country and himself,
And we must seek to right it as we may.
Meanwhile, have hence this rebel to the block;
Your lordship cannot privilege your head.
SPENCER SENIOR
Rebel is he that fights against his prince;   80
So fought not they that fought in Edward's right.
MORTIMER JUNIOR
Take him away; he prates.

                    [*Exit* SPENCER SENIOR, *guarded*]

                    You, Rhys ap Howell,
Shall do good service to her majesty,
Being of countenance in your country here,
To follow these rebellious runagates.   85
We in meanwhile, madam, must take advice
How Baldock, Spencer, and their complices
May in their fall be followed to their end.   *Exeunt*

[Scene 19]

Enter the ABBOT, MONKS,
[*King*] EDWARD, SPENCER [JUNIOR], *and* BALDOCK
[*, the latter three disguised as clergy*]

ABBOT
Have you no doubt, my lord, have you no fear;
As silent and as careful will we be
To keep your royal person safe with us,

---

78 *have hence* take away
79 Spencer Senior's newly acquired status saves him from hanging, but not
   decapitation.
80 *prince* ruler
84 *countenance* authority, influence
85 *runagates* (i) renegades (ii) traitors. In Elizabethan England the term was associated with voluntary Catholic exiles who were, it was thought, trained for sedition
   and assassination in the Continental seminaries.
86 *must take advice* i.e. consider, deliberate
87 *complices* accomplices
88 *followed to their end* i.e. pursued to their deaths

Free from suspect and fell invasion
Of such as have your majesty in chase –   5
Yourself, and those your chosen company –
As danger of this stormy time requires.

EDWARD

Father, thy face should harbour no deceit;
O hadst thou ever been a king, thy heart,
Pierced deeply with sense of my distress,   10
Could not but take compassion of my state.
Stately and proud, in riches and in train,
Whilom I was powerful and full of pomp;
But what is he, whom rule and empery
Have not in life or death made miserable?   15
Come Spencer, come Baldock, come sit down by me;
Make trial now of that philosophy
That in our famous nurseries of arts
Thou sucked'st from Plato and from Aristotle.
Father, this life contemplative is heaven –   20
O that I might this life in quiet lead!
But we, alas, are chased; and you, my friends,
Your lives and my dishonour they pursue.
Yet, gentle monks, for treasure, gold nor fee,
Do you betray us and our company.   25

MONKS

Your grace may sit secure, if none but we
Do wot of your abode.

SPENCER JUNIOR

Not one alive; but shrewdly I suspect
A gloomy fellow in a mead below;

---

4 *suspect* suspicion   *fell* cruel
5 *in chase* i.e. being pursued, hunted (like an animal in sport)
13 *Whilom* formerly
   pomp splendour, magnificence
14 *empery* dominion
18 *nurseries of arts* i.e. the universities of Oxford and Cambridge
20 *life contemplative* The 'contemplative life', as distinct from the 'active life' (both
   concepts derived from St Augustine's *City of God*), entailed religious devotion
   and solitude.
27 *wot* know
28 *shrewdly* intuitively
29 *gloomy fellow* the Mower, whom Spencer Junior supposes to be the figure of
   Death the Grim Reaper in the field, holding a scythe. Whilst this 'vision' adds
   to the tragic sense of foreboding, it may also suggest that Spencer Junior's
   imagination is being affected by exhaustion or fear.
   mead meadow
   below i.e. down, outside the abbey

A gave a long look after us, my lord,   30
And all the land, I know, is up in arms –
Arms that pursue our lives with deadly hate.
BALDOCK
We were embarked for Ireland, wretched we,
With awkward winds and sore tempests driven
To fall on shore and here to pine in fear   35
Of Mortimer and his confederates.
EDWARD
Mortimer! Who talks of Mortimer?
Who wounds me with the name of Mortimer,
That bloody man? [*He kneels*] Good father, on thy lap
Lay I this head, laden with mickle care.   40
O might I never open these eyes again,
Never again lift up this drooping head,
O never more lift up this dying heart!
SPENCER JUNIOR
Look up, my lord. Baldock, this drowsiness
Betides no good. Here even we are betrayed.   45

Enter, with Welsh hooks, RHYS AP HOWELL, *a* MOWER,
and the EARL OF LEICESTER[, *with soldiers*]

MOWER
Upon my life, those be the men ye seek.
RHYS AP HOWELL
Fellow, enough. [*To* LEICESTER] My lord, I pray be short;
A fair commission warrants what we do.
LEICESTER [*Aside*]
The Queen's commission, urged by Mortimer.
What cannot gallant Mortimer with the Queen?   50

---

34 *sore* harsh
35 *fall on shore* become grounded
39 *bloody* bloodthirsty, causing bloodshed
40 *mickle* much
44 *drowsiness* traditionally an ill omen
45 *Betides* bodes
45 sd 1 *Welsh hooks* scythe-like tools. Michael J. Warren convincingly argues that
   these are long-handled hedging-bills and not, as many editors have previously
   assumed, military weapons. This would make sense considering the presence of
   the Mower. See 'Welsh Hooks in *Edward II*', *N&Q*, n.s. 25 (1978), 109–10.
48 *fair commission* formal written authority
   warrants authorizes
50 *gallant* (i) bold (ii) lover

Alas, see where he sits and hopes unseen
T'escape their hands that seek to reave his life.
Too true it is: *quem dies vidit veniens superbum,*
Hunc dies vidit fugiens iacentem.
But Leicester, leave to grow so passionate.   55
[*Aloud*] Spencer and Baldock, by no other names,
I arrest you of high treason here.
Stand not on titles, but obey th'arrest;
'Tis in the name of Isabel the Queen.
My lord, why droop you thus?   60

EDWARD
O day! The last of all my bliss on earth,
Centre of all misfortune. O my stars!
Why do you lour unkindly on a king?
Comes Leicester, then, in Isabella's name
To take my life, my company, from me?   65
Here, man, rip up this panting breast of mine
And take my heart in rescue of my friends.

RHYS AP HOWELL
Away with them.

SPENCER JUNIOR   It may become thee yet
To let us take our farewell of his grace.

ABBOT
My heart with pity earns to see this sight;   70
A king to bear these words and proud commands!

EDWARD
Spencer, ah sweet Spencer, thus then must we part?

SPENCER JUNIOR
We must, my lord; so will the angry heavens.

EDWARD
Nay, so will hell and cruel Mortimer;

---

52 *reave* take away by force
53–4 *quem dies . . . iacentem* taken from Seneca's *Thyestes*, ll. 613–14. Translated by
    Jasper Heywood in 1560: 'Whom dawne of day hath seene in pryde to raygne, /
    Hym overthrowne hath seene the evening late.'
56 *no other names* Spencer Junior and Baldock are stripped of their recently acquired
    titles ('names').
58 *Stand* (i) assert (ii) rely on. The favourites are warned that they cannot expect
    the protection of noble privileges.
61–2 *O day . . . stars* Cf. 10. 4–5.
63 *lour* frown, look angry
66 *panting* (of the heart) palpitating
67 *rescue* release from legal custody
70 *earns* grieves
73, 74 *will* command, determine

The gentle heavens have not to do in this.   75
BALDOCK
My lord, it is in vain to grieve or storm.
Here humbly of your grace we take our leaves;
Our lots are cast. I fear me, so is thine.
EDWARD
In heaven we may, in earth never shall we meet.
And Leicester, say, what shall become of us?   80
LEICESTER
Your majesty must go to Kenilworth.
EDWARD
'Must'! 'Tis somewhat hard when kings must go.
LEICESTER
Here is a litter ready for your grace
That waits your pleasure; and the day grows old.
RHYS AP HOWELL
As good be gone, as stay and be benighted.   85
EDWARD
A litter hast thou? Lay me in a hearse,
And to the gates of hell convey me hence;
Let Pluto's bells ring out my fatal knell,
And hags howl for my death at Charon's shore,
For friends hath Edward none but these, and these,   90
And these must die under a tyrant's sword.
RHYS AP HOWELL
My lord, be going; care not for these,
For we shall see them shorter by the heads.
EDWARD
Well, that shall be shall be; part we must:

76 *storm* make a commotion
81 *Kenilworth* Q's old-spelling form, 'Killingworth', has an ominous aptness; some
    productions may wish to retain it in preference to the modernized version. See
    the Note on the Text for a full discussion of the modernization.
83 *litter* coach for one person which was usually carried by two men
85 i.e. it would be best to leave for Kenilworth before nightfall
88 *Pluto's bells* In classical mythology, Pluto was the keeper of the underworld and
    ruler of the dead. The bells were not part of classical tradition but probably rep-
    resent the death knell ringing out for those about to die.
89 *Charon* the ferryman of the classical underworld who transported the dead
    across the River Styx
90 *but these . . . these* This could be an implicit stage direction prompting Edward
    to gesticulate or point to Spencer Junior and Baldock.
93 i.e. they will be beheaded

Sweet Spencer, gentle Baldock, part we must.   95
Hence feignèd weeds, unfeignèd are my woes.
Father, farewell. Leicester, thou stay'st for me,
And go I must. Life, farewell with my friends.

Exeunt EDWARD *and* LEICESTER

SPENCER JUNIOR
O, is he gone? Is noble Edward gone,
Parted from hence, never to see us more?   100
Rend, sphere of heaven, and fire forsake thy orb!
Earth melt to air! Gone is my sovereign,   .
Gone, gone, alas, never to make return.
BALDOCK
Spencer, I see our souls are fleeted hence;
We are deprived the sunshine of our life.   105
Make for a new life, man; throw up thy eyes,
And heart and hand to heaven's immortal throne,
Pay nature's debt with cheerful countenance.
Reduce we all our lessons unto this:
To die, sweet Spencer, therefore live we all;   110
Spencer, all live to die, and rise to fall.
RHYS AP HOWELL
Come, come, keep these preachments till you come to the
place appointed. You, and such as you are, have made
wise work in England. Will your lordships away?

96 *feignèd* false
   weeds clothes. Cf. Peele's *Edward I*, 'Hence faigned weedes, unfaigned is my
   griefe' (2519)
101 *Rend* ed. (Rent Q) be torn apart
   sphere of heaven the Sun
104 *fleeted hence* i.e. have flown out of the body
105 *sunshine of our life* The King was frequently likened to the sun in Elizabethan
   drama. Cf. Shakespeare, *Richard II*, 3.3.61–2.
108 *Pay nature's debt* i.e. die; proverbial (Tilley D 168)
109 *Reduce* summarize
   lessons learning. Ironically, Baldock's last words recall his earlier scholastic
   pretensions.
110–11 Baldock resigns himself to death by reflecting that we are born to die; but
   his meditation also invokes the medieval 'de casibus' notion of tragedy in which
   an individual's rise to success is always followed by their fall.
112 *preachments* sermons
112–14 ed. (Come . . . till / you . . . appointed / You . . . in / England. / Will . . .
   away? Q)
113 *place appointed* i.e. the scaffold
113–14 *made . . . work* created havoc, caused trouble

MOWER
Your worship, I trust, will remember me?　　115
RHYS AP HOWELL
Remember thee, fellow? What else?
Follow me to the town.　　　　　　　[*Exeunt*]

[Scene 20]

Enter [EDWARD] *the King,* LEICESTER, *with the* BISHOP
[OF WINCHESTER, *and* TRUSSEL] *for the crown*[*, and
attendants*]

LEICESTER
Be patient, good my lord, cease to lament.
Imagine Kenilworth Castle were your court,
And that you lay for pleasure here a space,
Not of compulsion or necessity.
EDWARD
Leicester, if gentle words might comfort me,　　5
Thy speeches long ago had eased my sorrows,
For kind and loving hast thou always been.
The griefs of private men are soon allayed,
But not of kings: the forest deer, being struck,
Runs to an herb that closeth up the wounds;　　10
But when the imperial lion's flesh is gored,
He rends and tears it with his wrathful paw,
And, highly scorning that the lowly earth
Should drink his blood, mounts up into the air.
And so it fares with me, whose dauntless mind　　15
The ambitious Mortimer would seek to curb,
And that unnatural Queen, false Isabel,

---

115 i.e. will you reward me?
116 *What else?* But of course!

　0 sd ed. (*Enter the king, Leicester, with a Bishop | for the crowne.* Q)
　3 *lay* stayed, resided
　　　a space an interval, period of time
　8 *private men* i.e. those not holding public office
　　　allayed diluted, abated
9–10 *forest deer . . . wounds* Cf. the belief that the stag, when wounded by an arrow,
　　　would eat the herb dittany; this would close the wound, forcing the arrow
　　　out (Pliny, *Naturalis Historia* VIII.xli.97).
13 *And,* ed. not in Q
14 *mounts up* rises

That thus hath pent and mewed me in a prison.
For such outrageous passions cloy my soul,
As with the wings of rancour and disdain   20
Full often am I soaring up to heaven
To plain me to the gods against them both.
But when I call to mind I am a king,
Methinks I should revenge me of the wrongs
That Mortimer and Isabel have done.   25
But what are kings, when regiment is gone,
But perfect shadows in a sunshine day?
My nobles rule; I bear the name of King.
I wear the crown, but am controlled by them –
By Mortimer and my unconstant Queen   30
Who spots my nuptial bed with infamy,
Whilst I am lodged within this cave of care,
Where sorrow at my elbow still attends
To company my heart with sad laments,
That bleeds within me for this strange exchange.   35
But tell me, must I now resign my crown
To make usurping Mortimer a king?

BISHOP OF WINCHESTER
Your grace mistakes; it is for England's good
And princely Edward's right we crave the crown.

EDWARD
No, 'tis for Mortimer, not Edward's head,   40
For he's a lamb encompassèd by wolves
Which in a moment will abridge his life.
But if proud Mortimer do wear this crown,
Heavens turn it to a blaze of quenchless fire,

---

18 *pent* shut up
    mewed caged. Commonly used as a metaphor for imprisonment, a 'mew' was a
    cage or coop in which animals and birds were kept when being fattened for
    slaughter.
19 *outrageous* excessive
22 *plain* complain
26 *regiment* rule, power
27 *perfect* mere (Rowland)
30 *unconstant* unfaithful
34 *company* accompany
35 *strange exchange* i.e. the change of circumstances not becoming to a king
41 *lamb . . . by wolves* Cf. *3 Henry VI*, 'Such safety finds / The trembling lamb
    environèd with wolves' (1.1.242–3).
43–4 *crown . . . quenchless fire* Cf. Euripides' *Medea* (1186ff.) in which Jason deserts
    Medea for Creusa. Medea exacts her revenge by giving Creusa a golden crown
    which bursts into flames.

Or, like the snaky wreath of Tisiphon,   45
Engirt the temples of his hateful head;
So shall not England's vines be perishèd,
But Edward's name survives, though Edward dies.
LEICESTER
My lord, why waste you thus the time away?
They stay your answer: will you yield your crown?   50
EDWARD
Ah Leicester, weigh how hardly I can brook
To lose my crown and kingdom without cause,
To give ambitious Mortimer my right,
That like a mountain overwhelms my bliss;
In which extreme my mind here murdered is.   55
But what the heavens appoint, I must obey.

                        [*He removes his crown*]

Here, take my crown – the life of Edward too.
Two kings in England cannot reign at once.
But stay awhile; let me be King till night,
That I may gaze upon this glittering crown;   60
So shall my eyes receive their last content,
My head, the latest honour due to it,
And jointly both yield up their wishèd right.
Continue ever, thou celestial sun;
Let never silent night possess this clime.   65
Stand still, you watches of the element;
All times and seasons rest you at a stay,
That Edward may be still fair England's King.
But day's bright beams doth vanish fast away,
And needs I must resign my wishèd crown.   70
Inhuman creatures, nursed with tiger's milk,

---

45 *Tisiphon* Tisiphone, one of the Furies (see 4. 315 n.), whose hair was made of snakes

47 *vines* The vine was the emblem of regal lineage.

50 *stay* await

50–111 Shakespeare was substantially indebted to this passage in the deposition scene (4.1) of *Richard II.*

51 *weigh* ed. (way Q1–2; waigh Q3–4)

64–8 Cf. Faustus' last speech (*Dr Faustus*, 5.2) in which he desperately hopes to escape the mutable effects of time and forestall his imminent demise.

66 *watches . . . element* the stars and planets of the sky. The 'watches' are the four parts of the night, whilst the 'element' is the sky.

67 *rest . . . a stay* i.e. remain fixed

71 *tiger's milk* It was commonly believed that human moral characteristics were acquired from the mother through weaning; the tiger was a byword for cruelty.

Why gape you for your sovereign's overthrow?
My diadem, I mean, and guiltless life.
See, monsters, see, I'll wear my crown again.

[*He puts on the crown*]

What, fear you not the fury of your King?   75
But hapless Edward, thou art fondly led.
They pass not for thy frowns as late they did,
But seek to make a new-elected king,
Which fills my mind with strange despairing thoughts,
Which thoughts are martyred with endless torments;   80
And in this torment, comfort find I none
But that I feel the crown upon my head.
And therefore let me wear it yet a while.
TRUSSEL
My lord, the parliament must have present news,
And therefore say, will you resign or no?   85

                                The King rageth

EDWARD
I'll not resign, but whilst I live –
Traitors, be gone, and join you with Mortimer.
Elect, conspire, install, do what you will;
Their blood and yours shall seal these treacheries.
BISHOP OF WINCHESTER
This answer we'll return, and so farewell.   90

[*The* BISHOP OF WINCHESTER *and* TRUSSEL *begin to leave*]

LEICESTER
Call them again, my lord, and speak them fair,
For if they go, the Prince shall lose his right.
EDWARD
Call thou them back; I have no power to speak.
LEICESTER
My lord, the King is willing to resign.

---

76 *fondly* foolishly
77 *pass* care
   late i.e. recently
78 *seek* ed. (seekes Q)
86 The line is metrically short. Some editors emend to supply the missing foot ('be
   King'), but the Q reading can be interpreted as portraying Edward's exasperated
   inarticulacy.
88 *install* invest, place (someone) in authority

BISHOP OF WINCHESTER
  If he be not, let him choose –   95
EDWARD
  O would I might! But heavens and earth conspire
  To make me miserable.   [*He removes the crown*]
                    Here, receive my crown.
  Receive it? No, these innocent hands of mine
  Shall not be guilty of so foul a crime.
  He of you all that most desires my blood   100
  And will be called the murderer of a king,
  Take it. What, are you moved? Pity you me?
  Then send for unrelenting Mortimer
  And Isabel, whose eyes, being turned to steel,
  Will sooner sparkle fire than shed a tear.   105
  Yet stay, for rather than I will look on them,
  Here, here!   [*He gives the crown to the* BISHOP]
                    Now, sweet God of heaven,
  Make me despise this transitory pomp,
  And sit for aye enthronizèd in heaven,
  Come death, and with thy fingers close my eyes,   110
  Or if I live, let me forget myself.
BISHOP OF WINCHESTER
  My lord.
EDWARD
  Call me not lord! Away, out of my sight!
  Ah, pardon me; grief makes me lunatic.
  Let not that Mortimer protect my son;   115
  More safety is there in a tiger's jaws
  Than his embracements.   [*He gives a handkerchief*]
                    Bear this to the Queen,
  Wet with my tears and dried again with sighs.
  If with the sight thereof she be not moved,
  Return it back and dip it in my blood.   120
  Commend me to my son, and bid him rule
  Better than I. Yet how have I transgressed,

105 *sparkle fire* flash with anger or rage, like sparks struck from steel by friction
109 *for aye* for ever
     enthronizèd enthroned
111 ed. (*Enter Bartley* Q; sd moved to line 127 in this ed.
112 sp BISHOP OF WINCHESTER ed. (*Bartley* Q)
113–14 ed. (Call . . . lorde, / Away . . . me, / Greefe . . . lunatick, Q)
115 *protect* be Protector to
117 *Than* ed. (This Q)

Unless it be with too much clemency?

TRUSSEL
And thus, most humbly, do we take our leave.

EDWARD
Farewell. I know the next news that they bring   125
Will be my death, and welcome shall it be;
To wretched men death is felicity.

[*Enter* BERKELEY *with a letter*]

LEICESTER
Another post. What news brings he?

EDWARD
Such news as I expect. Come, Berkeley, come,
And tell thy message to my naked breast.   130

BERKELEY
My lord, think not a thought so villainous
Can harbour in a man of noble birth.
To do your highness service and devoir,
And save you from your foes, Berkeley would die.

LEICESTER [*Reading the letter*]
My lord, the council of the Queen commands   135
That I resign my charge.

EDWARD
And who must keep me now? Must you, my lord?

BERKELEY
Ay, my most gracious lord, so 'tis decreed.

EDWARD [*Taking the letter*]
By Mortimer, whose name is written here.

[*He tears up the letter*]

Well may I rend his name that rends my heart!   140
This poor revenge hath something eased my mind.
So may his limbs be torn, as is this paper!
Hear me, immortal Jove, and grant it too.

BERKELEY
Your grace must hence with me to Berkeley straight.

EDWARD
Whither you will; all places are alike,   145
And every earth is fit for burial.

---

130 *naked breast* Many editors argue that Edward is 'offering himself as to a murderer's dagger' (Gill).
131 sp BERKELEY ed. (*Bartley* Q; and throughout)
133 *devoir* duty
143 *Jove* or Jupiter, the supreme god in the Roman pantheon

LEICESTER
  Favour him, my lord, as much as lieth in you.
BERKELEY
  Even so betide my soul as I use him.
EDWARD
  Mine enemy hath pitied my estate,
  And that's the cause that I am now removed.   150
BERKELEY
  And thinks your grace that Berkeley will be cruel?
EDWARD
  I know not; but of this am I assured,
  That death ends all, and I can die but once.
  Leicester, farewell.
LEICESTER
  Not yet, my lord; I'll bear you on your way.   *Exeunt* 155

[Scene 21]

Enter MORTIMER [JUNIOR], *and Queen* ISABELLA

MORTIMER JUNIOR
  Fair Isabel, now have we our desire.
  The proud corrupters of the light-brained King
  Have done their homage to the lofty gallows,
  And he himself lies in captivity.
  Be ruled by me, and we will rule the realm.   5
  In any case, take heed of childish fear,
  For now we hold an old wolf by the ears,
  That if he slip will seize upon us both,
  And gripe the sorer, being griped himself.
  Think therefore, madam, that imports us much   10
  To erect your son with all the speed we may,
  And that I be Protector over him,
  For our behoof will bear the greater sway
  Whenas a king's name shall be underwrit.

149 *estate* condition
153 *I . . . once* proverbial (Tilley M 219)

  2 *light-brained* frivolous, wanton
  7 *hold . . . ears* proverbial (Tilley W 603)
  9 *gripe . . . sorer* i.e. will seize upon (us) more grievously
    griped afflicted
  10 *imports us much* i.e. it is most important for us (*us* ed.; as Q)
  11 *erect* establish on the throne
  13–14 i.e. Mortimer and the Queen will have greater authority when he can act in
    the King's name (literally, sign official documents as if he were the King)

ISABELLA
   Sweet Mortimer, the life of Isabel,   15
   Be thou persuaded that I love thee well,
   And therefore, so the Prince my son be safe,
   Whom I esteem as dear as these mine eyes,
   Conclude against his father what thou wilt,
   And I myself will willingly subscribe.   20
MORTIMER JUNIOR
   First would I hear news that he were deposed,
   And then let me alone to handle him.

Enter MESSENGER

MORTIMER JUNIOR
   Letters, from whence?
MESSENGER   From Kenilworth, my lord.
ISABELLA
   How fares my lord the King?
MESSENGER
   In health, madam, but full of pensiveness.   25
ISABELLA
   Alas, poor soul, would I could ease his grief.

    [*Enter the* BISHOP OF WINCHESTER *with the crown*]

   Thanks, gentle Winchester.
   [*To the* MESSENGER]   Sirrah, be gone.

                [*Exit* MESSENGER]

BISHOP OF WINCHESTER
   The King hath willingly resigned his crown.
ISABELLA
   O happy news! Send for the Prince, my son.
BISHOP OF WINCHESTER
   Further, ere this letter was sealed, Lord Berkeley came,   30
   So that he now is gone from Kenilworth.
   And we have heard that Edmund laid a plot
   To set his brother free; no more but so.
   The lord of Berkeley is so pitiful

---

18 *as dear . . . eyes* proverbial (Dent E 249)
19 *Conclude* i.e. make a final decision about the King's fate
22 *let me alone* trust me
25 *pensiveness* sadness, melancholy
30 sp BISHOP OF WINCHESTER ed. (*Bish* Q; and throughout the scene)
   ere ed. (*or* O)

As Leicester that had charge of him before.   35
ISABELLA
Then let some other be his guardian.

[*Exit* BISHOP OF WINCHESTER]

MORTIMER JUNIOR
Let me alone – here is the privy seal.
[*Calls offstage*] Who's there? Call hither Gourney and
    Maltravers.
To dash the heavy-headed Edmund's drift,
Berkeley shall be discharged, the King removed,   40
And none but we shall know where he lieth.
ISABELLA
But Mortimer, as long as he surviveo
What safety rests for us, or for my son?
MORTIMER JUNIOR
Speak, shall he presently be dispatched and die?
ISABELLA
I would he were, so it were not by my means.   45

Enter MALTRAVERS *and* GOURNEY

MORTIMER JUNIOR
Enough. Maltravers, write a letter presently
Unto the Lord of Berkeley from ourself,
That he resign the King to thee and Gourney;
And when 'tis done, we will subscribe our name.
MALTRAVERS
It shall be done, my lord.
MORTIMER JUNIOR   Gourney.
GOURNEY   My lord?   50
MORTIMER JUNIOR
As thou intendest to rise by Mortimer,
Who now makes Fortune's wheel turn as he please,

---

39 *dash* frustrate
    heavy-headed stupid, dull
    drift plot, scheme
43 *rests* remains
44 *dispatched* killed
48 *resign* surrender
52 *Fortune's wheel . . . please* In sixteenth-century iconography, Fortune was rep-
    resented with a wheel whose turning determined human fate; here Mortimer
    Junior arrogates that power to himself. Cf. *1 Tamburlaine*, 'I hold the Fates
    bound fast in iron chains / And with my hand turn Fortune's wheel about'
    (1.2.174–5).

Seek all the means thou canst to make him droop,
And neither give him kind word nor good look.
GOURNEY
I warrant you, my lord.   55
MORTIMER JUNIOR
And this above the rest, because we hear
That Edmund casts to work his liberty,
Remove him still from place to place by night,
And at the last he come to Kenilworth,
And then from thence to Berkeley back again.   60
And by the way to make him fret the more,
Speak curstly to him; and in any case
Let no man comfort him if he chance to weep,
But amplify his grief with bitter words.
MALTRAVERS
Fear not, my lord, we'll do as you command.   65
MORTIMER JUNIOR
So now away; post thitherwards amain.
ISABELLA
Whither goes this letter? To my lord the King?
Commend me humbly to his majesty,
And tell him that I labour all in vain
To ease his grief and work his liberty.   70
And bear him this, as witness of my love.

[She gives MALTRAVERS *a jewel]*

MALTRAVERS
I will, madam.

Exeunt MALTRAVERS *and* GOURNEY. ISABELLA
and MORTIMER [JUNIOR] *remain*

Enter the young PRINCE [EDWARD], *and the* EARL OF
KENT *talking with him*

MORTIMER JUNIOR [*Aside to* ISABELLA]
Finely dissembled; do so still, sweet Queen.
Here comes the young Prince with the Earl of Kent.
ISABELLA [*Aside to* MORTIMER JUNIOR]
Something he whispers in his childish ears.   75

57 *casts* plans
62 *curstly* malevolently, uncivilly
66 *post thitherwards amain* go there speedily
73 *dissembled* feigned

MORTIMER JUNIOR
  [Aside] If he have such access unto the Prince,
  Our plots and stratagems will soon be dashed.
ISABELLA
  [Aside] Use Edmund friendly, as if all were well.
MORTIMER JUNIOR
  How fares my honourable lord of Kent?
KENT
  In health, sweet Mortimer. How fares your grace?   80
ISABELLA
  Well – if my lord your brother were enlarged.
KENT
  I hear of late he hath deposed himself.
ISABELLA
  The more my grief.
MORTIMER JUNIOR
  And mine.
KENT
  [Aside] Ah, they do dissemble.   85
ISABELLA
  Sweet son, come hither; I must talk with thee.
MORTIMER JUNIOR
  Thou, being his uncle and the next of blood,
  Do look to be Protector over the Prince.
KENT
  Not I, my lord; who should protect the son
  But she that gave him life – I mean, the Queen?   90
PRINCE EDWARD
  Mother, persuade me not to wear the crown;
  Let him be King. I am too young to reign.
ISABELLA
  But be content, seeing it his highness' pleasure.
PRINCE EDWARD
  Let me but see him first, and then I will.
KENT
  Ay, do, sweet nephew.   95
ISABELLA
  Brother, you know it is impossible.
PRINCE EDWARD
  Why, is he dead?
ISABELLA
  No, God forbid.

81 *enlarged* released
92 *him* i.e. the Prince's father, Edward II

KENT
I would those words proceeded from your heart.

MORTIMER JUNIOR
Inconstant Edmund, dost thou favour him   100
That wast a cause of his imprisonment?

KENT
The more cause have I now to make amends.

MORTIMER JUNIOR
I tell thee 'tis not meet that one so false
Should come about the person of a prince.
My lord, he hath betrayed the King, his brother,   105
And therefore trust him not.

PRINCE EDWARD
But he repents and sorrows for it now.

ISABELLA
Come son, and go with this gentle lord and me.

PRINCE EDWARD
With you I will, but not with Mortimer.

MORTIMER JUNIOR
Why, youngling, 'sdain'st thou so of Mortimer?   110
Then I will carry thee by force away.

PRINCE EDWARD
Help, uncle Kent, Mortimer will wrong me.

            [*Exit* MORTIMER JUNIOR *with* PRINCE EDWARD]

ISABELLA
Brother Edmund, strive not; we are his friends.
Isabel is nearer than the Earl of Kent.

KENT
Sister, Edward is my charge; redeem him.   115

ISABELLA
Edward is my son, and I will keep him.   [*Exit*]

KENT
Mortimer shall know that he hath wrongèd me.
Hence will I haste to Kenilworth Castle
And rescue agèd Edward from his foes,
To be revenged on Mortimer and thee.   [*Exit*]

---

103 *meet* proper, appropriate
110 *youngling* stripling, novice (often spoken in a condescending manner)
      'sdain'st contracted form of 'disdainest'
115 *charge* responsibility   *redeem him* i.e. return him
119 *agèd Edward* Presumably the adjective serves to differentiate him from his son,
      Prince Edward; the historical Edward II was, at this point, only 43 years old.
120 sd ed. (*Exeunt omnes.* U)

[Scene 22]

Enter MALTRAVERS *and* GOURNEY [*carrying torches,*] *with*
[EDWARD] *the King*[*, and soldiers*]

MALTRAVERS
  My lord, be not pensive; we are your friends.
  Men are ordained to live in misery;
  Therefore come, dalliance dangereth our lives.
EDWARD
  Friends, whither must unhappy Edward go?
  Will hateful Mortimer appoint no rest?   5
  Must I be vexèd like the nightly bird
  Whose sight is loathsome to all wingèd fowls?
  When will the fury of his mind assuage?
  When will his heart be satisfied with blood?
  If mine will serve, unbowel straight this breast,   10
  And give my heart to Isabel and him;
  It is the chiefest mark they level at.
GOURNEY
  Not so, my liege; the Queen hath given this charge
  To keep your grace in safety.
  Your passions make your dolours to increase.   15
EDWARD
  This usage makes my misery increase.
  But can my air of life continue long
  When all my senses are annoyed with stench?
  Within a dungeon England's King is kept,
  Where I am starved for want of sustenance.   20
  My daily diet is heart-breaking sobs,
  That almost rends the closet of my heart.

1 *pensive* full of sorrow
3 *dalliance* idle delay
4 *unhappy* unfortunate
6 *vexèd* tormented
  nightly bird i.e. the owl (a common portent of death)
10 *unbowel* open up
  straight without delay
12 *mark* target
  level aim
17 *air of life* breath
22 *closet* private chamber

Thus lives old Edward, not relieved by any,
And so must die, though pitièd by many.
O water, gentle friends, to cool my thirst   25
And clear my body from foul excrements.
MALTRAVERS
Here's channel water, as our charge is given;
Sit down, for we'll be barbers to your grace.
EDWARD
Traitors, away! What, will you murder me,
Or choke your sovereign with puddle water?   30
GOURNEY
No, but wash your face and shave away your beard,
Lest you be known and so be rescuèd.
MALTRAVERS
Why strive you thus? Your labour is in vain.
EDWARD
The wren may strive against the lion's strength,
But all in vain; so vainly do I strive   35
To seek for mercy at a tyrant's hand.

> *They wash him with puddle water,*
> *and shave his beard away*

Immortal powers, that knows the painful cares
That waits upon my poor distressèd soul,
O level all your looks upon these daring men,
That wrongs their liege and sovereign, England's King.   40
O Gaveston, it is for thee that I am wronged;
For me, both thou and both the Spencers died,
And for your sakes a thousand wrongs I'll take.
The Spencers' ghosts, wherever they remain,
Wish well to mine; then tush, for them I'll die.   45
MALTRAVERS
'Twixt theirs and yours shall be no enmity.

---

26 *excrements* faeces. (The word also carried the archaic sense of 'hair', which
    Maltravers and Gourney take – by deliberate error – to be Edward's meaning.)
27 *channel* drain, sewer. Cf. 1. 187.
37–9 Forker compares Thomas Lodge's *Wounds of Civil War* (1588), 'Immortal
    powers that know the painful cares / That weight upon my poor distressed heart,
    / O bend your brows and level all your looks / Of dreadful awe upon these daring
    men.' (IV.ii.87–90).
44 *remain* dwell

Come, come away. Now put the torches out;
We'll enter in by darkness to Kenilworth.

Enter EDMUND [THE EARL OF KENT]

GOURNEY
How now, who comes there?
MALTRAVERS
Guard the King sure; it is the Earl of Kent.   50
EDWARD
O gentle brother, help to rescue me.
MALTRAVERS
Keep them asunder; thrust in the King.
KENT
Soldiers, let me but talk to him one word.
GOURNEY
Lay hands upon the Earl for this assault.
KENT
Lay down your weapons; traitors, yield the King!   55
MALTRAVERS
Edmund, yield thou thyself, or thou shalt die.

[*Soldiers seize* KENT]

KENT
Base villains, wherefore do you grip me thus?
GOURNEY
Bind him, and so convey him to the court.
EDMUND
Where is the court but here? Here is the King,
And I will visit him. Why stay you me?   60
MALTRAVERS
The court is where Lord Mortimer remains.
Thither shall your honour go; and so, farewell.

Exeunt MALTRAVERS *and* GOURNEY, *with* [EDWARD] *the*
King. EDMUND [THE EARL OF KENT] *and the soldiers*
[*remain*]

KENT
O, miserable is that commonweal, where lords
Keep courts and kings are locked in prison!

---

59 *Where . . . but here* In the sixteenth century the court was understood not only as
   a fixed location but as the establishment which accompanied the person of the
   King.
63 *commonweal* state

SOLDIER
Wherefore stay we? On, sirs, to the court.   65
KENT
Ay, lead me whither you will, even to my death,
Seeing that my brother cannot be released.   *Exeunt*

[Scene 23]

Enter MORTIMER [JUNIOR] *alone*

MORTIMER JUNIOR
The King must die, or Mortimer goes down;
The commons now begin to pity him.
Yet he that is the cause of Edward's death
Is sure to pay for it when his son is of age,
And therefore will I do it cunningly.   5
This letter, written by a friend of ours,
Contains his death, yet bids them save his life:
[*He reads*] '*Edwardum occidere nolite timere, bonum est*;
Fear not to kill the King, 'tis good he die.'
But read it thus, and that's another sense: 10
'*Edwardum occidere nolite, timere bonum est*;
Kill not the King, 'tis good to fear the worst.'
Unpointed as it is, thus shall it go,
That, being dead, if it chance to be found,
Maltravers and the rest may bear the blame,   15
And we be quit that caused it to be done.
Within this room is locked the messenger
That shall convey it and perform the rest.
And by a secret token that he bears,
Shall he be murdered when the deed is done.   20
Lightborne, come forth.

[*Enter* LIGHTBORNE]

Art thou as resolute as thou wast?

---

13 *Unpointed* unpunctuated. The letter's meaning is made ambiguous through its lack of punctuation; this is intended to obscure Mortimer Junior's involvement in Edward's death.

14 *being dead* i.e. once Edward is murdered

16 *quit* acquitted, exonerated

21 *Lightborne* The assassin derives from theatrical and not historical sources; such characters were popular in tragedies of the late 1580s and early 1590s. It is significant that he shares his name (which Anglicizes Lucifer) with one of Satan's associates in the Chester cycle of mystery plays (c. 1467–88): according to a well-known saying of the time, 'An Englishman Italianate is the Devil incarnate.'

LIGHTBORNE
What else, my lord? And far more resolute.
MORTIMER JUNIOR
And hast thou cast how to accomplish it?
LIGHTBORNE
Ay, ay, and none shall know which way he died.
MORTIMER JUNIOR
But at his looks, Lightborne, thou wilt relent.   25
LIGHTBORNE
Relent? Ha, ha! I use much to relent.
MORTIMER JUNIOR
Well, do it bravely, and be secret.
LIGHTBORNE
You shall not need to give instructions;
'Tis not the first time I have killed a man.
I learned in Naples how to poison flowers,   30
To strangle with a lawn thrust through the throat,
To pierce the windpipe with a needle's point,
Or, whilst one is asleep, to take a quill
And blow a little powder in his ears,
Or open his mouth and pour quicksilver down.   35
But yet I have a braver way than these.
MORTIMER JUNIOR
What's that?
LIGHTBORNE
Nay, you shall pardon me; none shall know my tricks.
MORTIMER JUNIOR
I care not how it is, so it be not spied.
Deliver this to Gourney and Maltravers.   40

[*He gives the letter to* LIGHTBORNE]

---

26 *use much* i.e. am accustomed to (spoken facetiously)

27 *bravely* (i) without fear (ii) excellently, finely

30–6 *I learned . . . these* Lightborne's account of his studies in Naples – reputedly the most dangerous of Italian cities – may recall a panic of late 1591 about a trained Italian assassin being sent to England to assassinate the Queen; see Introduction, p. xv. Cf. also *The Jew of Malta*, 'I learned in Florence how to kiss my hand' (2.3.23), 'I walk abroad a-nights / And kill sick people groaning under walls; / Sometimes I go about and poison wells . . .' (2.3.175–7).

31 *lawn . . . throat* a piece of fine linen cloth forced down the victim's throat to block the windpipe

34 *powder in his ears* Cf. the murder of Hamlet's father in Shakespeare's play (1.5.61–70).

35 *quicksilver* mercury (which is poisonous)

36 *braver* more skilful

38 *tricks* skills, methods

At every ten miles' end thou hast a horse.
[*Giving a token*] Take this. Away, and never see me more.
LIGHTBORNE
No?
MORTIMER JUNIOR
No, unless thou bring me news of Edward's death.
LIGHTBORNE
That will I quickly do. Farewell, my lord.   [*Exit*]   45
MORTIMER JUNIOR
The Prince I rule, the Queen do I command,
And with a lowly congé to the ground
The proudest lords salute me as I pass;
I seal, I cancel, I do what I will.
Feared am I more than loved; let me be feared,   50
And when I frown, make all the court look pale.
I view the Prince with Aristarchus' eyes,
Whose looks were as a breeching to a boy.
They thrust upon me the protectorship
And sue to me for that that I desire.   55
While at the council table, grave enough,
And not unlike a bashful Puritan,
First I complain of imbecility,
Saying it is *onus quam gravissimum*,
Till being interrupted by my friends,   60
Suscepi that *provinciam*, as they term it,
And to conclude, I am Protector now.
Now is all sure: the Queen and Mortimer

---

42 *Take this* i.e. the 'secret token' (19) which will seal Lightborne's fate
47 *congé* bow
49 *seal* authorize official documents
50 *Feared . . . feared* Mortimer Junior follows the advice of Machiavelli's *The Prince*,
    a forbidden book of the period which circulated surreptitiously in manuscript:
    'because hardly can [love and fear] subsist both together, it is much safer to be
    feared, than to be lov'd' (XVII, trans. Edward Dacres, London, 1640, p. 130).
52 *Aristarchus* notoriously harsh schoolmaster and grammarian who lived in
    Alexandria in the second century B.C.
53 *breeching* whipping
55 *sue to* petition
57 *Puritan* follower of an extreme Protestant movement which emerged in the six-
    teenth century and was theologically rooted in Calvinism. Puritans were known
    for their hypocritical advocacy of self-restraint.
58 *imbecility* weakness
59 *onus quam gravissimum* (Latin) a very heavy burden
61 *Suscepi . . . provinciam* (Latin) I have undertaken that office

Shall rule the realm, the King, and none rule us.
Mine enemies will I plague, my friends advance,   65
And what I list command, who dare control?
Maior sum quam cui possit fortuna nocere.
And that this be the coronation day,
It pleaseth me, and Isabel the Queen.

[Trumpets sound within]

The trumpets sound; I must go take my place.   70

*Enter the young King [EDWARD III], BISHOP [OF
CANTERBURY], CHAMPION, NOBLES, [and] Queen
[ISABELLA]*

BISHOP OF CANTERBURY
Long live King Edward, by the grace of God,
King of England and Lord of Ireland.
CHAMPION
If any Christian, Heathen, Turk, or Jew
Dares but affirm that Edward's not true King,
And will avouch his saying with the sword,   75
I am the Champion that will combat him.   *[Silence]*
MORTIMER JUNIOR
None comes. Sound trumpets.   *[Trumpets sound]*
KING EDWARD III   Champion, here's to thee.

[He raises his goblet]

ISABELLA
Lord Mortimer, now take him to your charge.

Enter SOLDIERS with the EARL OF KENT prisoner

MORTIMER JUNIOR
What traitor have we there with blades and bills?
SOLDIER
Edmund, the Earl of Kent.
KING EDWARD III   What hath he done?   80
SOLDIER
A would have taken the King away perforce,

---

66 *list* desire to
67 *Maior sum quam cui possit fortuna nocere* I am so great that Fortune cannot harm
me; from Ovid's *Metamorphoses*, VI. 195
71 sp BISHOP OF CANTERBURY ed. (*Bish.* Q)
77 sp KING EDWARD III ed. (*King.* Q; and throughout)
79 *blades and bills* swords and halberds
81 *perforce* by force, violently

As we were bringing him to Kenilworth.

MORTIMER JUNIOR
Did you attempt his rescue, Edmund? Speak.

KENT
Mortimer, I did; he is our King,
And thou compell'st this prince to wear the crown.   85

MORTIMER JUNIOR
Strike off his head! He shall have martial law.

KENT
Strike off my head? Base traitor, I defy thee.

KING EDWARD III
My lord, he is my uncle and shall live.

MORTIMER JUNIOR
My lord, he is your enemy and shall die.

KENT
Stay, villains.   90

KING EDWARD III
Sweet mother, if I cannot pardon him,
Entreat my Lord Protector for his life.

ISABELLA
Son, be content; I dare not speak a word.

KING EDWARD III
Nor I, and yet methinks I should command;
But seeing I cannot, I'll entreat for him.   95
My lord, if you will let my uncle live,
I will requite it when I come to age.

MORTIMER JUNIOR
'Tis for your highness' good, and for the realm's.
[To soldiers] How often shall I bid you bear him hence?

KENT
Art thou King? Must I die at thy command?   100

MORTIMER JUNIOR
At our command. Once more, away with him.

KENT
Let me but stay and speak; I will not go.
Either my brother or his son is King,
And none of both them thirst for Edmund's blood.

---

86 *martial law* (here) summary execution without trial
101 *our command* The text is ambiguous: the emphasis on 'our' can suggest
    Mortimer's responsible action as Protector, jointly with the Queen; but it can
    also suggest his overweening ambition in adopting the royal plural.
104 *none of both them* ed. (none of both, then Q) i.e. neither of them

And therefore, soldiers, whither will you hale me?   105

> *They hale* EDMUND [THE EARL OF KENT] *away,*
> *and carry him to be beheaded*

> [*Exit* MORTIMER JUNIOR *with attendants,* BISHOP OF
> CANTERBURY, NOBLES, CHAMPION. KING EDWARD III *and*
> ISABELLA *remain*]

KING EDWARD III
What safety may I look for at his hands,
If that my uncle shall be murdered thus?
ISABELLA
Fear not, sweet boy, I'll guard thee from thy foes.
Had Edmund lived, he would have sought thy death.
Come son, we'll ride a-hunting in the park.   110
KING EDWARD III
And shall my uncle Edmund ride with us?
ISABELLA
He is a traitor; think not on him. Come.   *Exeunt*

[Scene 24]

Enter MALTRAVERS *and* GOURNEY

MALTRAVERS
Gourney, I wonder the King dies not,
Being in a vault up to the knees in water,
To which the channels of the castle run,
From whence a damp continually ariseth
That were enough to poison any man,   5
Much more a king, brought up so tenderly.
GOURNEY
And so do I, Maltravers. Yesternight
I opened but the door to throw him meat,
And I was almost stifled with the savour.
MALTRAVERS
He hath a body able to endure   10
More than we can inflict; and therefore now
Let us assail his mind another while.
GOURNEY
Send for him out thence, and I will anger him.

4 *damp* fog, mist
8 *meat* food
9 *savour* smell, stench

Enter LIGHTBORNE

MALTRAVERS
  But stay, who's this?
LIGHTBORNE   My Lord Protector greets you.

          [*He presents them with the letter*]

GOURNEY
  What's here? I know not how to construe it.   15
MALTRAVERS
  Gourney, it was left unpointed for the nonce:
  [*Reading*] 'Edwardum occidere nolite timere' –
  That's his meaning.
LIGHTBORNE [*Showing the token*]
  Know you this token? I must have the King.
MALTRAVERS
  Ay, stay a while; thou shalt have answer straight.   20
  [*Aside to* GOURNEY] This villain's sent to make away the
    King.
GOURNEY
  [*Aside to* MALTRAVERS] I thought as much.
MALTRAVERS [*Aside to* GOURNEY]   And when the
    murder's done,
  See how he must be handled for his labour.
  Pereat iste! Let him have the King.
  What else? [*To* LIGHTBORNE] Here is the keys; this is the   25
    lake.
  Do as you are commanded by my lord.
LIGHTBORNE
  I know what I must do; get you away –
  Yet be not far off; I shall need your help.
  See that in the next room I have a fire,
  And get me a spit, and let it be red hot.   30
MALTRAVERS
  Very well.
GOURNEY
  Need you anything besides?

13 sd ed.; after line 14 in Q
16 *unpointed* unpunctuated
    for the nonce for the purpose in hand
21 *make away* i.e. murder
24 *Pereat iste!* Let him die!
25 *lake* dungeon; also associated with hell. Cf. *2 Tamburlaine*, 'And travel headlong
    to the lake of hell' (3.5.24).

LIGHTBORNE
  What else? A table and a featherbed.
GOURNEY
  That's all?
LIGHTBORNE
  Ay, ay; so when I call you, bring it in.   35
MALTRAVERS
  Fear not you that.
GOURNEY
  Here's a light to go into the dungeon.

                    [*Exit* MALTRAVERS *and* GOURNEY]

LIGHTBORNE
  So now must I about this gear; ne'er was there any
  So finely handled as this king shall be.
  Foh! Here's a place indeed with all my heart.   40

                    [*Enter* EDWARD]

EDWARD
  Who's there? What light is that? Wherefore comes thou?
LIGHTBORNE
  To comfort you and bring you joyful news.
EDWARD
  Small comfort finds poor Edward in thy looks.
  Villain, I know thou com'st to murder me.
LIGHTBORNE
  To murder you, my most gracious lord?   45
  Far is it from my heart to do you harm.
  The Queen sent me to see how you were used,
  For she relents at this your misery.
  And what eyes can refrain from shedding tears

---

33 *featherbed* stuffed palliasse; see notes on ll. 71 and 112
38 *about* i.e. proceed with, get on with
   gear business
40 *Foh!* Lightborne is affected by the stench of the dungeon.
   with all my heart i.e. I must say (Bevington and Rasmussen)
40 sd Q gives no stage direction for Edward to enter, which may indicate that the
   entry was unconventional and possibly not under the prompter's direct control.
   An attractive possibility is that the dungeon is imagined to be located in the
   under-stage area (often referred to as 'hell'), and that Lightborne reveals Edward
   by opening a trapdoor at line 40; he would then emerge through it at some point
   in the ensuing dialogue. (Line 58 suggests that he is no longer in his dungeon.)
   Alternatively, some editors have assumed that he is 'discovered', i.e. revealed
   when a traverse curtain is drawn back at the rear of the stage.
47 *used* i.e. being treated

To see a king in this most piteous state?   50
EDWARD
    Weep'st thou already? List awhile to me,
    And then thy heart, were it as Gourney's is,
    Or as Maltravers', hewn from the Caucasus,
    Yet will it melt ere I have done my tale.
    This dungeon where they keep me is the sink   55
    Wherein the filth of all the castle falls.
LIGHTBORNE
    O villains!
EDWARD
    And there in mire and puddle have I stood
    This ten days' space; and lest that I should sleep,
    One plays continually upon a drum.   60
    They give me bread and water, being a king,
    So that for want of sleep and sustenance
    My mind's distempered and my body's numbed,
    And whether I have limbs or no, I know not.
    O, would my blood dropped out from every vein,   65
    As doth this water from my tattered robes.
    Tell Isabel the Queen I looked not thus
    When for her sake I ran at tilt in France
    And there unhorsed the Duke of Cleremont.
LIGHTBORNE
    O speak no more, my lord; this breaks my heart.   70
    Lie on this bed and rest yourself awhile.
EDWARD
    These looks of thine can harbour nought but death.
    I see my tragedy written in thy brows.
    Yet stay awhile; forbear thy bloody hand,
    And let me see the stroke before it comes,   75
    That even then when I shall lose my life,

51 *List* listen
53 *Caucasus* the mountain range between the Black and Caspian Seas known for its harsh terrain and bitterly cold climate
55 *sink* cess-pool
56 *filth* sewage
63 *distempered* deranged, mentally disturbed
64 *no* not
68–9 an invented incident not recounted in the chronicles
68 *ran at tilt* jousted
71 *this bed* i.e. the 'featherbed' called for by Lightborne at line 33. The text gives no indication of how and when the prop should be brought on stage.
73 *tragedy* destruction
76 *That even* ed. (That and euen Q)

My mind may be more steadfast on my God.
LIGHTBORNE
What means your highness to mistrust me thus?
EDWARD
What means thou to dissemble with me thus?
LIGHTBORNE
These hands were never stained with innocent blood,   80
Nor shall they now be tainted with a king's.
EDWARD
Forgive my thought, for having such a thought.
One jewel have I left; receive thou this.
Still fear I, and I know not what's the cause,
But every joint shakes as I give it thee.   85
O if thou harbour'st murder in thy heart,
Let this gift change thy mind and save thy soul.
Know that I am a king – O, at that name,
I feel a hell of grief. Where is my crown?
Gone, gone. And do I remain alive?   90
LIGHTBORNE
You're overwatched, my lord; lie down and rest.
EDWARD
But that grief keeps me waking, I should sleep;
For not these ten days have these eyes' lids closed.
Now as I speak they fall, and yet with fear
Open again. O wherefore sits thou here?   95
LIGHTBORNE
If you mistrust me, I'll be gone, my lord.
EDWARD
No, no, for if thou mean'st to murder me,
Thou wilt return again, and therefore stay.

                                        [*He falls asleep*]

LIGHTBORNE
He sleeps.
EDWARD
[*Starting*] O let me not die! Yet stay, O stay awhile.   100
LIGHTBORNE
How now, my lord?

---

83 *One jewel* possibly the jewel sent by the Queen at 21. 71; if so, Edward's hand-
      ing it over to another potential favourite would be his final act of betrayal
89–90 *Where . . . remain alive* A king without a crown is usually dead.
91 *overwatched* depleted through lack of sleep
92 *grief* anxiety

EDWARD
Something still buzzeth in mine ears
And tells me, if I sleep I never wake.
This fear is that which makes me tremble thus;
And therefore tell me, wherefore art thou come?   105
LIGHTBORNE
To rid thee of thy life. Maltravers, come!

[*Enter* MALTRAVERS]

EDWARD
I am too weak and feeble to resist;
Assist me, sweet God, and receive my soul.
LIGHTBORNE
Run for the table.   [*Exit* MALTRAVERS]

[*Enter* MALTRAVERS *with* GOURNEY, *carrying a table and hot spit*]

EDWARD
O spare me, or dispatch me in a trice!   110
LIGHTBORNE
So, lay the table down and stamp on it;
But not too hard, lest that you bruise his body.

[*They seize* EDWARD *and hold him down, laying the table on him.*
LIGHTBORNE *murders him with the spit. He screams and dies*]

MALTRAVERS
I fear me that this cry will raise the town,
And therefore let us take horse and away.
LIGHTBORNE
Tell me, sirs, was it not bravely done?   115

102 *buzzeth* whispers
109 sd 2 The 'featherbed' asked for at line 33 is already on stage, mentioned at line
71. Some editors treat that 'bed' as a separate prop, and have the featherbed for
the murder brought on here. However, the effect of giving the two actors another
bulky object to carry is unreasonably to slow down the action at a climactic
point, with no covering dialogue provided by the text.
112 sd On the staging of this moment see the Introduction. The text gives no indication as to how Lightborne uses the featherbed he asked for. It probably serves
as a buffer to prevent bruising by direct contact with the table; if Edward is lying
on it immediately beforehand, the murderers must first pitch him onto the
ground. Alternatively, Lightborne may want it not for the murder itself but to
offer Edward comfort, and so a false sense of security, during their preceding
conversation.
115 *bravely* skilfully

GOURNEY
Excellent well. Take this for thy reward.

Then GOURNEY *stabs* LIGHTBORNE

Come, let us cast the body in the moat,
And bear the King's to Mortimer, our lord.
Away!   *Exeunt*[, *carrying the bodies*]

[Scene 25]

Enter MORTIMER [JUNIOR] *and* MALTRAVERS

MORTIMER JUNIOR
Is't done, Maltravers, and the murderer dead?
MALTRAVERS
Ay, my good lord; I would it were undone.
MORTIMER JUNIOR
Maltravers, if thou now growest penitent
I'll be thy ghostly father; therefore choose
Whether thou wilt be secret in this,   5
Or else die by the hand of Mortimer.
MALTRAVERS
Gourney, my lord, is fled, and will, I fear,
Betray us both; therefore let me fly.
MORTIMER JUNIOR
Fly to the savages!
MALTRAVERS
I humbly thank your honour.   [*Exit*]   10
MORTIMER JUNIOR
As for myself, I stand as Jove's huge tree,
And others are but shrubs compared to me.
All tremble at my name, and I fear none;
Let's see who dare impeach me for his death.

Enter [ISABELLA] *the Queen*

ISABELLA
Ah, Mortimer, the King my son hath news   15
His father's dead, and we have murdered him.

118–19 ed. (*one line in* Q)
119 sd ed. (*Exeunt omnes.* Q)

4 *ghostly father* priest (who hears the confessions of those about to die)
9 *to the savages* i.e. beyond civilization, to the wilderness
11 *Jove's huge tree* the oak, a byword for size and steadfastness

MORTIMER JUNIOR
What if he have? The King is yet a child.
ISABELLA
Ay, ay, but he tears his hair and wrings his hands,
And vows to be revenged upon us both.
Into the council chamber he is gone   20
To crave the aid and succour of his peers.

Enter the King [EDWARD III], *with the* LORDS [*and*
attendants]

Ay me, see where he comes, and they with him.
Now, Mortimer, begins our tragedy.
FIRST LORD
Fear not, my lord; know that you are a king.
KING EDWARD III
Villain!   25
MORTIMER JUNIOR
How now, my lord?
KING EDWARD III
Think not that I am frighted with thy words.
My father's murdered through thy treachery,
And thou shalt die; and on his mournful hearse
Thy hateful and accursèd head shall lie   30
To witness to the world that by thy means
His kingly body was too soon interred.
ISABELLA
Weep not, sweet son.
KING EDWARD III
Forbid not me to weep; he was my father.
And had you loved him half so well as I,   35
You could not bear his death thus patiently.
But you, I fear, conspired with Mortimer.
FIRST LORD
Why speak you not unto my lord the King?
MORTIMER JUNIOR
Because I think scorn to be accused.
Who is the man dare say I murdered him?   40

---

17 *yet* still
21 *succour* support
21 sd ed.; after line 23 in Q
24 sp FIRST LORD ed. (*Lords.* Q; also at ll. 38 and 93)
36 *patiently* calmly

KING EDWARD III
  Traitor, in me my loving father speaks
  And plainly saith, 'twas thou that murd'redst him.
MORTIMER JUNIOR
  But hath your grace no other proof than this?
KING EDWARD III
  Yes, if this be the hand of Mortimer.

                              [*He presents the letter*]

MORTIMER JUNIOR [*Aside to* ISABELLA]
  False Gourney hath betrayed me and himself.   45
ISABELLA [*Aside to* MORTIMER JUNIOR]
  I feared as much; murder cannot be hid.
MORTIMER JUNIOR
  'Tis my hand; what gather you by this?
KING EDWARD III
  That thither thou didst send a murderer.
MORTIMER JUNIOR
  What murderer? Bring forth the man I sent.
KING EDWARD III
  Ah, Mortimer, thou knowest that he is slain;   50
  And so shalt thou be too. Why stays he here?
  Bring him unto a hurdle, drag him forth;
  Hang him, I say, and set his quarters up!
  But bring his head back presently to me.
ISABELLA
  For my sake, sweet son, pity Mortimer.   55
MORTIMER JUNIOR
  Madam, entreat not; I will rather die
  Than sue for life unto a paltry boy.
KING EDWARD III
  Hence with the traitor, with the murderer.
MORTIMER JUNIOR
  Base Fortune, now I see that in thy wheel

---

41 *in me . . . speaks* 'Marlowe carefully withholds this final show of authority in the
   young prince until, at this point, at the death of his father, he is king in legal fact'
   (Merchant).
46 *murder cannot be hid* proverbial (Tilley M 1315)
52 *hurdle* frame or sledge which restrained traitors whilst being dragged through the
   streets to the place of execution
53 Mortimer Junior is to be hanged, drawn, and quartered rather than merely beheaded, the normal privilege of aristocratic traitors granted even to Gaveston,
   Baldock, and the Spencers.

There is a point to which, when men aspire,   60
They tumble headlong down; that point I touched,
And seeing there was no place to mount up higher,
Why should I grieve at my declining fall?
Farewell, fair Queen. Weep not for Mortimer,
That scorns the world, and as a traveller   65
Goes to discover countries yet unknown.

KING EDWARD III
What! Suffer you the traitor to delay?

[*Exit* MORTIMER JUNIOR, *with the* FIRST LORD *and guard*]

ISABELLA
As thou received'st thy life from me,
Spill not the blood of gentle Mortimer.

KING EDWARD III
This argues that you spilt my father's blood,   70
Else would you not entreat for Mortimer.

ISABELLA
I spill his blood? No!

KING EDWARD III
Ay, madam, you; for so the rumour runs.

ISABELLA
That rumour is untrue; for loving thee
Is this report raised on poor Isabel.   75

KING EDWARD III
I do not think her so unnatural.

SECOND LORD
My lord, I fear me it will prove too true.

KING EDWARD III
Mother, you are suspected for his death,
And therefore we commit you to the Tower
Till further trial may be made thereof;   80
If you be guilty, though I be your son,
Think not to find me slack or pitiful.

ISABELLA
Nay, to my death, for too long have I lived
Whenas my son thinks to abridge my days.

KING EDWARD III
Away with her. Her words enforce these tears,   85

---

75 *report* rumour
     raised i.e. fabricated against
77 sp SECOND LORD (*Lords.* Q; also at ll. 89 and 91)
80 *trial* investigation
84 *abridge* shorten, cut short
85 *enforce* produce, cause

And I shall pity her if she speak again.

ISABELLA
Shall I not mourn for my belovèd lord,
And with the rest accompany him to his grave?

SECOND LORD
Thus, madam, 'tis the King's will you shall hence.

ISABELLA
He hath forgotten me; stay, I am his mother.   90

SECOND LORD
That boots not; therefore, gentle madam, go.

ISABELLA
Then come, sweet death, and rid me of this grief.

[*Exit* ISABELLA, *guarded*]

[*Enter* FIRST LORD *with the head of* MORTIMER JUNIOR]

FIRST LORD
My lord, here is the head of Mortimer.

KING EDWARD III
Go fetch my father's hearse, where it shall lie,
And bring my funeral robes.   [*Exit attendants*]
                          Accursèd head!   95
Could I have ruled thee then, as I do now,
Thou hadst not hatched this monstrous treachery.

[*Enter attendants with the hearse of King* EDWARD II
and funeral robes]

Here comes the hearse; help me to mourn, my lords.
Sweet father, here unto thy murdered ghost
I offer up this wicked traitor's head.   100
And let these tears, distilling from mine eyes,
Be witness of my grief and innocency.

[*Exeunt, with a funeral march*]

---

91 *boots* avails, matters
101 *distilling* falling from (in small droplets)
102 Colophon omitted ed. (FINIS. / [Device] / Imprinted at London for *William* /
Ihones, *and are to be solde at his* / shop, neere vnto Houlburne / *Conduit.* 1594. Q)